MIND IMPROVEMENT

for beginners

This book includes:

LEARN FASTER

HOW TO ANALYZE PEOPLE

DARK PSYCHOLOGY FOR BEGINNERS

Tony Brain

© **Copyright 2019 by Tony Brain -** *All rights reserved.*

No part of this guide may be reproduced in any form without permission in writing from the publisher except in the case of brief quotations embodied in critical articles or reviews.

Legal & Disclaimer

The information contained in this book and its contents is not designed to replace or take the place of any form of medical or professional advice; and is not meant to replace the need for independent medical, financial, legal or other professional advice or services, as may be required. The content and information in this book has been provided for educational and entertainment purposes only.

The content and information contained in this book has been compiled from sources deemed reliable, and it is accurate to the best of the Author's knowledge, information and belief. However, the Author cannot guarantee its accuracy and validity and cannot be held liable for any errors and/or omissions. Further, changes are periodically made to this book as and when needed. Where appropriate and/or necessary, you must consult a professional (including but not limited to your doctor, attorney, financial advisor or such other professional advisor) before using any of the suggested remedies, techniques, or information in this book.

Upon using the contents and information contained in this book, you agree to hold harmless the Author from and against any damages, costs, and expenses, including any legal fees potentially resulting from the application of any of the information provided by this book. This disclaimer applies to any loss, damages or injury caused by the use and application, whether directly or indirectly, of any advice or information presented, whether for breach of contract, tort, negligence, personal injury, criminal intent, or under any other cause of action.

You agree to accept all risks of using the information presented inside this book.

You agree that by continuing to read this book, where appropriate and/or necessary, you shall consult a professional (including but not limited to your doctor, attorney, or financial advisor or such other advisor as needed) before using any of the suggested remedies, techniques, or information in this book.

TABLE OF CONTENTS

BOOK #1: LEARN FASTER - How to Improve Yourself and Master Your Memory with Advanced Learning Strategies..........9

INTRODUCTION..........11

PART I TEACH YOURSELF TO LEARN..........13

CHAPTER 1: CHANGE YOUR MINDSET TO BE OPEN TO LEARNING..........15

CHAPTER 2: THE PLEASURE OF LEARNING - How and Why We Find Joy in Gaining Knowledge..........33

CHAPTER 3: BRAIN FOOD - How to Fuel the Brain For Mental Acuity..........47

CHAPTER 4: ANATOMY OF THE BRAIN - How the Hippocampus Works for Long - and Short- Term Memory..........65

CHAPTER 5 THE IMPORTANCE OF PRACTICE - Using Study and Hard Work to Produce Gratifying Results..........83

CHAPTER 6: INEFFECTIVE TECHNIQUES AND LEARNING MYTHS- How NOT to Train the Brain...105

CHAPTER 7: THE POMODORO TECHNIQUE - How to Ignore Distractions to Better Manage Your Study Time..........117

PART II TECHNIQUES FOR LASTING LEARNING..................125

CHAPTER 8: SPEED READING - Picking Up the Pace for Faster Reading and Comprehension.....................127

CHAPTER 9: SELECTIVE LEARNING - The Art of Discerning What Information Is Necessary................141

CHAPTER 10: NAMES AND NUMBERS - Tricks for Memorizing Everyday Things.......................................151

CHAPTER 11: MIND MAPPING - Using Visualization to Make Memorable Connections..............................165

CHAPTER 12: AN ELEPHANT NEVER FORGETS - Learn Like a Pachyderm for Better Retention............173

CHAPTER 13: MEMORY PALACE - Building a Mental Castle for Your Mnemonic Devices............................183

CHAPTER 14: 80/20 - Using the Pareto Principle to Maximize Your Learning Efforts.................................199

CONCLUSION..215

BOOK #2: HOW TO ANALYZE PEOPLE How to Read and Influence People with the Ultimate Guide to Reading Body Language and Nonverbal Communication..219

INTRODUCTION..221

Chapter 1: Reading People Through Their Handwriting..229

Chapter 2: Uncovering Insights About Values............245

Chapter 3: Analyzing People Through Their Environment..259

Chapter 4: Judging by the Cover................................271

Chapter 5: Reading People Through Their Photographs..283

Chapter 6: Identifying Deception Through Nonverbal Clues..297

Chapter 7: Body Language of Attraction....................315

Chapter 8: Ultimate Nonverbal Clue Cheat Sheet.....323

Chapter 9: Communication to Read People...............351

Chapter 10: Effective Tips and Tricks for Reading People..367

Chapter 11: Personality and Birth Order....................385

Chapter 12: Body Language Reading Tips To Slay Your Next Negotiation..403

Chapter 13: Recognizing Personality Type..................411

Conclusion..427

BOOK #3: DARK PSYCHOLOGY_FOR BEGINNERS What are the Secrets of Mind Manipulation and Control?..431

Introduction...433

Chapter 1: What is the Dark Psychology Story?..........437

Chapter 2: The dark core of personality/Dark Factor of Personality..447

Chapter3: Case Studies..459

Chapter4: Manipulation..479

Chapter5: NLP (Neuro-Linguistic Programming).....497

Chapter6: How to defend from people with the dark side of personality: narcissism, sadism, etc.................521

Conclusion..541

Bibliography/Sources..545

LEARN FASTER

How to Improve Yourself and
Master Your Memory with
Advanced Learning Strategies

INTRODUCTION

Thank you for choosing LEARN FASTER: *How to Improve Yourself and Master Your Memory with Advanced Learning Strategies.* This book will provide you a comprehensive overview of learning methodology and practical ways to apply those methods. In the following pages, you'll discover techniques for improving your memory, increasing your studying power, and training yourself to learn more efficiently.

In Part I, you will get an overview of what it takes to learn, from preparing yourself and your study space, to how the brain and body work together to retain information. There's a chapter about how the brain processes how memories are formed and what foods you can consume to fuel your brain power. You'll also learn about time management and how misconceptions about learning can affect your progress.

In Part II, you'll learn about time-tested learning techniques and methods for speed reading, mind mapping and creating memory palaces. You will also learn how to use mnemonic devices to remember just about anything, and how to tackle having a poor memory for names and numbers. Part II also includes information on maximizing your efforts in studying, and how to apply what you've learned to all aspects of your life.

Along the way, you'll find plenty of examples and exercises to help you practice these techniques. These exercises have been designed to reinforce concepts and create new learning habits. Practice, as they say, makes perfect! Spending just a short amount of time each day on these exercises can boost your mental performance and help you LEARN FASTER.

So put your thinking cap on, dive in, and enjoy!

PART I

TEACH YOURSELF TO LEARN

CHAPTER 1
CHANGE YOUR MINDSET TO BE OPEN TO LEARNING

"A mind is like a parachute. It doesn't work if it is not open."
— Frank Zappa

Learning is a life-long process, despite what the adage says about old dogs and new tricks. Children in school are constantly faced with new knowledge, which they absorb, and which then becomes integrated into their memories. So why is it that as adults, that type of learning seems to become more difficult?

It may be because children's young brains are still developing and forming neural pathways.

Once humans reach adulthood, those neural pathways are set, and eventually they will begin to deteriorate. The mature human brain is already filled with memories and experiences. Learning new skills can feel daunting, because adult brains are seemingly 'out of room.'

The truth is, adult learning doesn't have to be difficult or seen as a chore. It is completely possible to reroute those neural pathways, create new ones, and develop constructive habits which will assist the learning process. Opening yourself up to new educational opportunities and adopting a positive attitude is are the first steps towards successful learning.

What Is the End Goal?

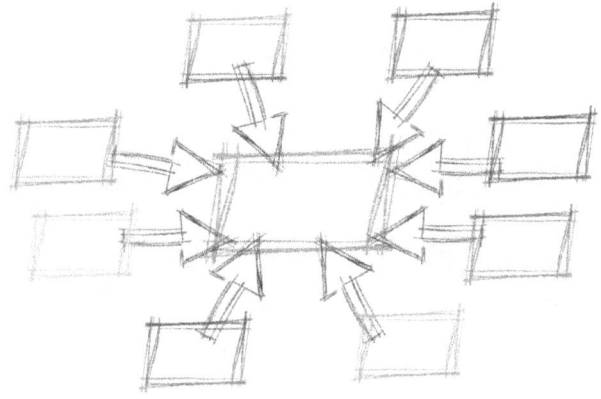

Before anyone can undertake any brain-training or academic study, it's important to determine the desired outcome. Do you want to have a better memory, or have you always wanted the ability to speed-read? Are you looking to improve your study skills? Adult learners these days often find themselves in need of continuing education to further their careers, or make the decision to change career paths entirely and realize they are in need of training. It's important to identify the end goal of any educational undertaking *before* getting started.

What Is the Best Way to Learn?

Learning anything new requires the ability to receive and retain information. People learn in different ways, from childhood through adulthood, and that can change as a person ages. Someone who could learn quite well audibly (through retaining information they'd been told) as a youth may have grown into an adult who is a visual learner, needing to see or read the information for themselves. Still others are kinesthetic learners, meaning they retain knowledge through tactile, hands-on methods. While most people learn through a combination of styles, it will always be easier to acquire new knowledge if you know your preferred method of learning.

Exercise: Write down five random nouns, and on a separate piece of paper, draw simple pictures that represent five different random nouns. Study the list of words and the drawings for a short time, about 2-3 minutes apiece. Put the notes away, and wait for 24 hours. After a full day, try to first recall the five written words and then the five drawings. Did you remember more of the words or the drawings? Did you learn more by reading and writing, or by drawing and doing? To test your audible learning skills, have someone else read you a list of random words. Again, wait 24 hours and see how well you recall the list.

There *is* a caveat to learning styles, as some recent studies will suggest. While knowing what style of learning works best for you is a wonderful tool, you'll still have to be flexible in your learning and put in the hard work of studying. Some experts say that to truly learn, a variety of study material works best to stave away boredom. This isn't to say learning styles are invalid, it is to say that sometimes you may have to watch a film when you'd rather read, or put in the extra effort on a hands-on project when you'd rather not. It's all a part of opening yourself up to learning.

Ask, "Am I Personally Ready to Learn?"

Preparing to acquire any new skill or knowledge doesn't have to be nerve-wracking. By identifying your educational goal and your primary learning style, you've begun to set yourself up for success. Be open-minded and practical about your goals. Rome, as they say, wasn't built in a day, and a brain doesn't get rewired overnight. Studying and learning takes effort. Habits are built and broken over days and weeks, and sometimes even months and years.

Don't despair if you've never been the best student! In this book, you'll discover a myriad of techniques to benefit all kinds of learners. The most important thing is to be willing and eager. Maybe you've heard of some of the methods outlined here, and thought to yourself, "There's no way that will work for me!" But if you maintain an open mind and an enthusiastic attitude, there's nothing you can't learn and no strategy you can't employ.

Open Yourself Up to New Things

Do you remember as a child being told to try a new food? Maybe your mother even said, "Try it! You'll like it!" Sometimes you tried it and it was delicious, and sometimes you flat out refused. Fast forward twenty years, and you decide to try that same food as an adult. Turns out, that food is amazing! Isn't it a shame that you wasted two decades thinking you didn't like it?

The point is, you'll never know if you like anything until you've tried it, and you don't know just how much you can learn until you put your mind to it. Going into a task convinced that you'll fail will set you up for failure. Many of the learning techniques in this book are best practiced if you consider your brain to be a blank slate.

When you are open minded about learning, you can find yourself achieving things you may never have thought possible. Maintaining an open mind allows you to be more receptive of new concepts, gives you a better understanding of opposing or contrasting points of view, and helps you to be more confident in your ability to learn.

Being an open minded learner will also strengthen your critical thinking skills. While discovering a new learning technique is wonderful, being able to apply it beyond basic exercises is the key to making the technique a permanent part of your psyche. After all, if you can't apply the method in everyday life, what good is it to you, and what have you really learned?

The Building Blocks of Learning and Confidence

When small children learn to read, they don't go immediately from cardboard picture books to *War and Peace*. Becoming a confident reader takes plenty of time and practice, and it is a beautiful thing to watch a toddler sounding out their first words grow into an elementary-schooler who can read sentences and understand context. Adult learning functions in much the same way, but without a doting parent or a favorite teacher to mark milestones, there isn't nearly as much applauding and encouragement going on. Adult learners need to be their own cheerleaders to become more confident in their skills.

Breaking down learning tasks into small segments can be a great way to measure your achievements against your goals. If you are working on a skill in which you've never had any experience, make a list of the components of that skill and work on one component at a time until you can put them all together. The satisfaction of reaching those small milestones will keep up your learning momentum and motivate you to hit the next mark. Several of the following chapters will touch upon this skill, which is known as 'chunking'.

You should also confide in someone about your goals, like a partner or spouse, or your friends or family. You can ask them to provide you encouragement through the learning process. If you are working to improve your memory, tell them what techniques you're using and ask for assistance if necessary. Maybe you'd like help with flashcards or lists, or maybe you need to ask your partner to allow you a little quiet study time every day. No matter your goal, sharing it with your loved ones will hold you accountable and provide you with a support system. Hearing positive feedback and encouraging words will help you become more confident in your skills.

Consider the Practice of Mindfulness

We've all heard of the term 'mindfulness', but what does it really mean and how can you apply it to become a stronger, faster learner? Mindfulness is a state of awareness, of being in tune with your senses, and of being able to focus on the present moment and on a precise task. It's also about having the ability to self-regulate your actions and emotions to maintain an open mind and a sense of curiosity.

Have you ever felt like you did a sleepwalk through an everyday task? We've all driven somewhere on autopilot, or had a 'did I close the garage door?' moment. Chances are good that you did indeed close the garage door, because it's part of a routine so ingrained that you don't *have* to think about it. When we go about our business in the same way every day, we tend to lose awareness of what we're actually doing.

To actively practice mindfulness is to take the time to focus on each moment as it occurs. Instead of getting in your car and thinking about a hundred other things on the way to the office, think about the feel of the steering wheel in your hands. Look at the bright colors of the traffic lights, or count off how many stop signs you navigate through on your daily route. You'll be surprised to find how little you know about what's found in the distance between your home and workplace.

There are other ways to practice mindfulness, including mindful meditation. If you can incorporate just a few minutes of mindfulness into each day, you'll find yourself feeling calmer, more open-minded and clear-headed, and better able to focus on necessary tasks, including learning. The great thing about practicing mindfulness is that it doesn't cost anything, except for a little bit of your time. Here's how to get started:

Set aside the time- It's important to dedicate time if you want to practice mindfulness. It doesn't have to be very long, maybe 10 or 15 minutes every day. Once you've become experienced at mindful meditation, you can adjust the time you spend on it each day. You'll begin to know how much time you need.

Find a quiet place- If you want to be able to focus and clear your head, it's important to have a place where you can do so, where you can be uninterrupted and sit peacefully.

Be comfortable- Be sure that you're physically comfortable when you have your mindfulness sessions. Have a cozy place to sit, wear unrestrictive clothing, and make sure the temperature is adjusted properly. The idea is to reduce any physical distractions so that you can focus on the mental exercise of mindfulness.

Breathe easy- You want to calm your brain by focusing on your breathing. Feel each breath, and try to keep it even and steady.

Pay attention to your body- Think about how your body feels as you are sitting still. Can you feel your heart beating? Are your arms and legs comfortably at rest? Try to make yourself aware of how every inch of your body feels.

Don't wander away- Whenever you feel your thoughts starting to wander, bring yourself back to the point of focusing on your breath. Don't get mad at yourself for daydreaming- the purpose of mindfulness is not to completely empty your head. You just want to teach yourself to focus. You can go back to the steady breathing step and start over.

Be nice to yourself- It takes time to get the hang of mindfulness. Don't give up if you find your brain wandering more than you think it should be. The more you practice mindfulness, the better you will get at it.

Studies show that people who practice mindfulness have increased concentration and better memories. Those who practice mindfulness also have less stress and anxiety, sleep better, and have greater cognitive function. There also seems to be a link between mindfulness and slowing the progression of Alzheimer's disease. Students who practice mindfulness perform better on standardized tests and report a greater capacity to retain information.

Get Excited About Adult Learning

Of course, one of the best things about learning as an adult is that the subject matter can be anything you wish! There's no standard curriculum in the school of life, so if you want to teach yourself to speedread or learn to improve your memory, do it! If you want to learn logic puzzles or how to paint watercolors, do that, too! The possibilities are endless with adult learning, and this book will give you the skills to learn anything you want. You don't have to be like our poor friend Calvin- you aren't bound by the constraints of a first-grade syllabus.

The learning skills you'll find in these pages will help you better understand the complexities of memory and retention, and will aid you in any field you intend to study. Gaining new knowledge is human nature; it's what moved our species from the Stone Age through the Industrial Revolution to the technological era of today. It's one of the most wonderful things about humans...we will always be hungry for the next big advancement in learning and growth.

CHAPTER 2
THE PLEASURE OF LEARNING - How and Why We Find Joy in Gaining Knowledge

"Learning never exhausts the mind."
-Leonardo da Vinci

Learning is fun. Repeat that again. Learning is fun. The constant chase for knowledge drives the human race to unimaginable heights. It's taken us to the depths of the oceans and into the reaches of outer space. The human thirst for knowledge has put men on the moon, discovered millions of species alive and extinct, and keeps the bastions of higher education in business. But why? What is it about learning that gives people so much pleasure?

Biology Plays a Key Role

Humans are, at their core, competitive creatures. Tens of thousands of years ago, survival of the fittest was the law of the land. The man who could hunt the largest beast, make the sharpest spear, run the fastest and climb the highest was more likely to survive to pass his DNA to the next generation. It took skill, cunning, and innovation to live long enough to reproduce. The competition we see today in education, sport, and business stems from that early human biology.

The human race is hardwired to learn, to grow, and to advance. When we are children, we acquire new skills without a conscious thought. A baby naturally progresses from sitting, to crawling, to standing, then walking. Schoolchildren develop new skills under the watchful guidance of their teachers, and it often doesn't take long before they discover which are their favorite subjects. As adults with the freedom to follow our interests, learning never has to be a chore.

Finding Your Path to Learning

Once you've figured out your learning style, you can best decide how to make studying work for you. If you find that you're a visual learner, books and videos may be your best option. The advent of audiobooks are a boon for audible learners, and hands-on, or kinesthetic, learners may benefit from workshops or seminars.

Technology today allows for endless options at endless price points to achieve any learning goal. Libraries carry more books than ever these days and have become multimedia resources for those on a budget, offering e-books, computer access, educational programming and electronic materials. Today's libraries are a wealth of resources beyond traditional materials.

Many local colleges and cooperative extensions offer free or low-cost courses and one-day offerings. Webinars abound on nearly any subject you can think of, and can be found with a just a little online research. With such an abundance of educational opportunities, it's easier than it's ever been to find something new to learn about and find a resource to enable you to do so.

Why Does Learning Feel So Good?

Have you ever read something you need to mull over in your brain for a few moments? Then it clicks! You have a marvelous 'aha!' moment, and you can't help but smile. That 'aha!' moment has just released some endorphins, which are the human body's feel-good neurotransmitter. The more 'aha!' moments that you have, the more endorphins that will be released.

Studies show that if you are already in a good mood, and therefore releasing endorphins, *before* you begin to study, you'll actually learn faster. Activities like exercising or listening to music before studying can raise your endorphin levels and aid your learning process.

Dopamine plays a role in learning, too. This is another of the brain's 'happy' neurotransmitters. This chemical is released when you're feeling pleasure, and is kicked into high gear by being in a good mood. It's also released when you eat dark chocolate, but eating excessive amounts of sugar before studying probably isn't the best method! Maybe just one or two pieces, though…

When we feel the kick of endorphins, we're driven to want to keep that feeling alive. It's why a child doesn't want to leave a birthday party, or why we don't want a wonderful night out with friends to end. When you say, "I'm just having too much fun," what that means on a biological level is that your endorphins are high, you're feeling great, and your body doesn't want that feeling to fade.

Does this mean that the human brain can actually get addicted to learning? In a way, yes. Human beings are creatures prone to addictions, and it's proven that addiction changes the chemistry and make-up of our brains. When we hear that, we're quick to jump to the negative side of addiction. Alcohol and substance dependency can and do have ravaging effects on the makeup and function of the brain. Behavioral addictions like gambling also create these negative effects. Exercise and brain training have the opposite effect; they can build healthier brain tissue.

Is Any Addiction a GOOD Addiction?

We've all heard the term 'runner's high'. That's the effect caused by pushing the body through enough physical activity for the brain to release a surge of endorphins and dopamine. Can mental activity produce the same effect? The simple answer is yes. Pushing yourself to learn can activate the same chemicals. Once the body becomes used to these chemicals being present, it will become conditioned to want more. This is addiction, on its most basic level.

The difference between this type of addiction and addictions to unhealthy substances or behaviors comes down the effects on the brain and body. Exercise builds healthy tissue, stronger muscles, and increases the flow of oxygen to the brain. Exercise has also been shown to increase activity in the hippocampus, which is the part of the brain known to affect memory and learning. Later in this book, we will examine the hippocampus and its memory functions in depth.

Learning itself has a positive effect on the brain. The endorphins produced during those 'aha!' moments creates a desire to continue feeling good. It's shown that learning begets learning- once you've created that connection, you'll want to make the next one, and the next. In fact, the more you learn, the more you *can* learn, and you'll begin learning faster. So in a way, your own brain forms a 'good addiction' to the learning process.

Our Ever-changing Brains

On the biological level, the act of learning creates what's known as 'brain plasticity'. The brain is a constantly changing organ; it is made up of a mass of chemicals and cellular tissue and electrical activity. The healthy human brain is never stagnant, but is a nearly unimaginable number of cells in constant motion. When we learn, the brain adapts to include the new knowledge or skill. What's happening at the cellular level is that the brain is making new synaptic connections.

These connections can also help your brain build myelin, a protective material that coats the axons, or transmission cells, in the tissue. The erosion of myelin is linked to diseases which affect neurological function, most notably multiple sclerosis. The reduction of myelin also plays a role in the brain function of patients afflicted with Alzheimer's disease and Parkinson's disease.

The brain is a wondrous machine. It is a powerhouse; it's a memory vault; it's a speech center, and so much more. It's the organ that regulates the rest of our organs. If learning can increase its function and its productivity, *and* protect against potentially devastating disease, then learning should be an activity to be embraced and practiced regularly.

The Competition Factor

Early in this chapter, we briefly touched upon the innate competitive nature of humans. Why do schools depend on grading systems? Why do they hand out awards, and why do they name a valedictorian? Because it feels so good to succeed. Successful students aren't always necessarily the smartest students, but they are the ones who are willing to work hard to receive recognition. Being recognized for effort and achievement is yet another thing which releases those endorphins. In short, winning feels good, in and beyond the academic arena.

Competition in the adult world is what fuels business and innovation. Successful corporations are made up of people who are smart, savvy, and most importantly, willing to learn and adapt in a rapidly changing global economic climate. Those who cannot learn and grow will be left behind.

Scientific advances are also being made every day by people who are devoted life-long learners. Diseases are being cured, food is being engineered to feed more people, and the outer reaches of space are being explored using man-made equipment developed over centuries of discovery and experimentation. These advances wouldn't exist without people who are open to learning and those who are persistent in their pursuit of greater knowledge.

Turning Failures into Successes

One of the other joys we can take from learning is the joy of failure. Yes, that sounds counterintuitive, but failure can fuel big success. We've all heard stories of big name athletes who were cut from their high school squads, notably the inspirational tale of Michael Jordan being cut from his varsity basketball team. He really showed them, huh?

People who can learn from their failures are people who can analyze what went wrong, and turn the situation around into something that goes wildly right. By learning what their weakness was, finding a solution to improve upon it, and using that knowledge to become first proficient and then superior in those skills, failure is turned into success.

Approaching perceived failure as a learning tool is a healthy way to keep yourself motivated. It goes back to that ingrained need for competition, and sometimes the person we need to compete with the most is our self. Integrating the self-reflection discussed in the first chapter with the biological factors covered in this one is a great way to get on the road to meeting your learning goals.

Another way you can take your learning to the next level is by eating foods that have a positive effect on your brain health. In the next chapter, we'll take a look at some of the food groups that have the most benefit for your brain and how to incorporate them into your diet.

CHAPTER 3
BRAIN FOOD - How to Fuel the Brain For Mental Acuity

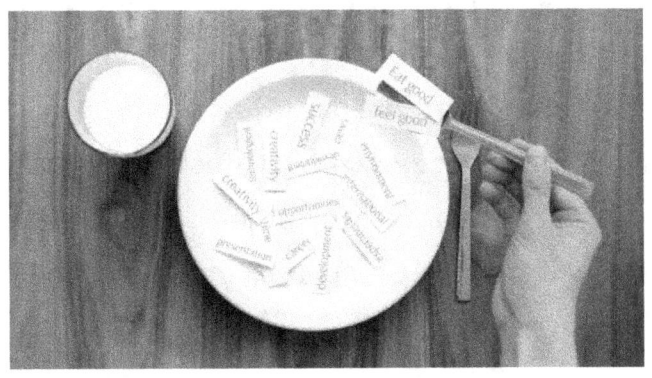

"First we eat, then we do everything else."
- MFK Fisher

Remember being told as a child that "breakfast is the most important meal of the day"? While it's rumored that the adage was a conspiracy dreamt up by breakfast cereal companies to sell more sugary morsels to young families, there's no denying that it's more difficult to concentrate when we are hungry.

We absolutely need to fuel our bodies and our brains in order to be able to learn. But is there truth to some of the wives' tales about eating breakfast to start the day? How about carrots improving your eyesight, or is fish really brain food? Let's examine what it takes to really feed yourself, and your brain cells for maximum learning power.

What Does the Brain Need to Eat?

In order to determine the foods that make the best brain food, let's break down the organ itself a little bit. What does the brain need to perform at its best?

The human brain is made up of two types of specialized cells, categorized as either grey matter or white matter. The grey matter is composed of neurons, and the white matter is made up of cells called axons and dendrites, which all serve to transmit the electrical energy which sends message through the brain. The axons, as previously mentioned, are coated in myelin sheaths, which protect the cells.

The neurons are the gatherers of the brain. They collect and store the information that will be turned into the messages the axons transmit. About 60 percent or more of the brain is made up of fatty tissue, which makes it the fattiest organ in the human body. The brain also uses up about 20 percent of daily calorie intake.

So, how do we nourish an organ that needs so much fuel and is also made of cells unlike any others? We can consume foods that are rich in antioxidants, omega-3 fatty acids, and cruciferous vegetables like leafy greens. These foods can provide the brain with proper fuel for daily activities and high performance tasks.

It's True! Fish Really *is* Brain Food

Omega-3 fatty acids are a fatty compound found in nature, but which the human body cannot produce on its own. This 'good fat' is found in fish, in some nuts, and in eggs and dairy. The consumption of foods which are rich in omega-3s has been linked to lower cholesterol and better heart health.

When it comes to the brain, that's where omega-3 fatty acids do the hard work. There are three main types of omega-3s. DHA (docosahexaenoic acid) is found in fatty fishes and fish oil. This compound is a crucial building block for brain cells, and also affects the retinas of the eyes. For people who choose not to eat fish, there are many commercially available fish oil supplements. DHA is also found in the meat, dairy, and eggs harvested from grass-pastured livestock.

ALA (alpha-linolenic acid) is another key omega-3 fatty acid, and this one comes primarily from plant-based sources. This compound can be found in nuts like walnuts, and in seeds like flax and chia, which have become very popular in the recent decade. Soybeans are also a good source of ALA. EPA (eicosapentaenoic acid) is the third omega-3 fatty acid. EPA can also be found in fish and fish oil, and more importantly, the human body can convert EPA into DHA.

Antioxidants Against Free Radicals

Free radicals are the toxic waste of the body. Free radicals are made up of cellular byproducts that clog up the bloodstream, and they can cause damage to healthy tissue if not removed or neutralized. Antioxidants, a class of substances which can slow down or prevent damage from free radicals, are crucial for brain health. Antioxidants are found in a wide variety of foods, mostly plant-based.

Antioxidants play a vital role in brain health, cleaning up free radicals and preventing and reversing the oxidative stress they cause. Oxidative stress occurs when the body cannot neutralize free radicals at a fast enough pace, and cell damage occurs. When oxidative stress is allowed to progress unchecked, oxidative damage results. Oxidative damage is linked to such diseases as Parkinson's and Alzheimer's. This damage can also have a negative effect on heart health, and is also known to be involved in genetic mutation disorders like Fragile X Syndrome.

When we consume enough antioxidants, it can help increase blood flow and oxygen flow to the brain. Increasing intake of antioxidants has been shown to have a positive effect on reversing memory loss. Some antioxidants are so helpful in inhibiting the development of Alzheimer's disease, they have become part of a recommended Alzheimer's Prevention diet.

There are two categories of antioxidants, flavonoids and non-flavonoids. Flavonoids are plant-based antioxidant compounds, found in things like tea, cocoa, and grapes, and the pigmentation found in brightly colored vegetables. Non-flavonoids are things like vitamins A, C, and E, and minerals like selenium and manganese. As a general rule, the more colorful the food is, the more antioxidants that food contains.

Foods which contain antioxidants in high levels are known as superfoods. These include vegetables like kale and artichokes, and berries like acai and goji. If these varieties of produce aren't readily available in your area, don't be too concerned. Many other veggies and berries are also rich in antioxidants; consider things like eggplant, tomatoes, or spinach, or blueberries and strawberries.

Cooking can affect the antioxidant level in some foods. Tomatoes will release the antioxidant lycopene in more readily useable form when heated, but foods like peas and cauliflower actually lose their antioxidant powers when cooked. Try to eat these vegetables raw, if possible, or cook very briefly. Steaming and blanching are good methods to prevent the leaching of antioxidants.

Cruciferous Vegetables

Cruciferous vegetables are a large family of plants which includes cauliflower, broccoli, cabbage, kale, bok choy, and arugula, among many others. These vegetables are not only high in antioxidants, they are shown to have positive effects on language skills, memory, and attention span.

Dark leafy greens are also high in Vitamin A, having nearly 400 percent the recommended daily amount per serving. Vitamin A is key in organ health and development, including that of the brain.

Spice Things Up!

Your spice rack is another great source of brain-healthy foodstuffs. There's a multitude of spices which can provide antioxidants or have been shown to increase or repair cognitive abilities. So the next time you're cooking, try adding basil, rosemary, or thyme for their anti-inflammatory and antioxidant properties. Eating garlic, which is a standard in most kitchens, is a great way to promote and increase health blood flow to the brain. Turmeric, oregano, and cinnamon all have brain-health benefits, too, like staving off Alzheimer's, increasing memory power and concentration, and protecting brain cells from damage.

Making Sure Enough is Enough

Eating for a healthy brain doesn't have to be complicated, and it doesn't have to be boring, either. There are so many foods with a positive effect on the brain, so there are sure to be meals to fit every budget and taste. Talking to your doctor about supplements is also a viable option for adding omega-3 fatty acids, antioxidants, and vitamins into your health regimen. You don't have to spend a fortune to improve your brain health through food consumption.

Keep It Light...

While it's important to eat for brain health, it's also important not to weigh yourself down. Eat small meals made up of foods that will keep you feeling full longer, rather than large, heavy meals that will lower your energy levels. It's much easier to concentrate on learning task when you are fueled up, satisfied, and alert.

And **Keep It Interesting**

With such a wide variety of brainy foods available, try mixing up your menu with lots of fresh produce, quality meat products, and whole grains. Try playing around with the sample menus below:

Breakfast: Scrambled eggs (or egg whites) and fresh berries, whole wheat toast

Snack: Almonds and dried cranberries

Lunch: Arugula salad with chopped walnuts and a light vinaigrette

Snack: Raw carrots and cucumbers

Dinner: Salmon, quinoa, and steamed green beans

Dessert: 2 oz. of dark chocolate (60 percent or higher cacao)

Or:

Breakfast: Whole grain oat cereal with low-fat milk and strawberries

Snack: Roasted peanuts

Lunch: Tuna salad on whole wheat

Snack: Low-fat mozzarella cheese and olives

Dinner: Grass-fed beef burger, sweet potato fries

Dessert: Fresh pineapple, grilled and sprinkled with cinnamon

Foods on the Flip Side

Just as there are a variety of foods that promote brain health and better learning, there are many foods that have a negative effect. That isn't to say you need to eliminate these foods completely, but it's best to eat them in smaller quantities or in moderation. Let's look at the list of brain-busting culprits:

Processed meats and cheeses- Bacon and other smoked meats, tinned or canned cheese spreads, and other overly processed deli products contain nitrogen byproducts like nitrites and nitrosamines. These compounds can cause the liver to produce fatty toxins which affect the brain. These types of foods have also been linked to increased risk of Alzheimer's disease.

'White foods'- Carbohydrate products which have been processed to take out all natural color and imperfection are also not conducive to good brain health. This would include things like white bread, white rice, pastas and noodles, or other items made from bleached flours or sugars. These foods spike the body's blood sugars, forcing insulin production which then affects the brain.

Microwave popcorn- This beloved convenience treat contains diacetyl, a chemical compound which is known to attack the amyloid tissues in the brain, increasing the potential for neurological disorders like Alzheimer's or Parkinson's diseases. Diacetyl is also found in some margarines.

Artificial sweeteners- Compounds like aspartame, found in many diet soft drinks, and other artificial sweeteners are found to have a link to dementia and stroke. It's believed the chemicals in artificial sweeteners block neurotransmitters in the brain. Excessive consumption of aspartame has also been linked to irritability and depression.

Trans-fats- Natural trans-fats are found in minimally processed foods, but trans-fats become an issue with overconsumption of manufactured products like shortening, prepackaged baked goods, margarine, and other junk foods. Studies have shown that trans-fats are detrimental to brain health by causing lower cognitive capacity and less memory capacity. Trans-fats are also not good for heart health, which also has a direct effect on blood flow to the brain.

Alcohol- Chronic alcohol misuse is shown to have negative effects on brain health by disrupting the flow of neurotransmitters, leading to decreased memory and cognitive function. Alcohol use in young people whose brains are still developing can cause abnormal brain function, and pregnant women should avoid alcohol, which can damage the growing brain of the fetus. Even people who do not abuse alcohol every day, but binge-drink when they do, show a decreased level of activity in key function centers of the brain.

Fish which have high mercury levels- Mercury, a heavy metal, builds up in the tissue of certain fish, such as swordfish. The toxins produced by consuming too much mercury can disrupt the production of neurotransmitters. Pregnant women, especially, should avoid eating fish that are typically found to carry a lot of mercury.

Drinks high in sugar- Most sugary drinks are sweetened with high fructose corn syrup. HFCS can cause inflammation in the brain, and excessive consumption can lead to metabolic disorders, like Type 2 diabetes, which can also negatively affect the brain, and which has been linked to Alzheimer's and dementia.

Feel Good About Your Brain Fuel

When it comes to choosing foods that will fuel your brain, you'll find those same foods fuel your body in a positive way as well. Remember that not all food is created equal. Look for quality ingredients, and eat a wide variety to avoid taste bud boredom. You'll find that half the fun in feeding your brain is coming up with new and exciting flavor combinations. Once you've fueled yourself up for brain health, you'll be ready to take on the next chapter where we'll be tackling the physiology of memory.

CHAPTER 4
ANATOMY OF THE BRAIN - How the Hippocampus Works for Long - and Short- Term Memory

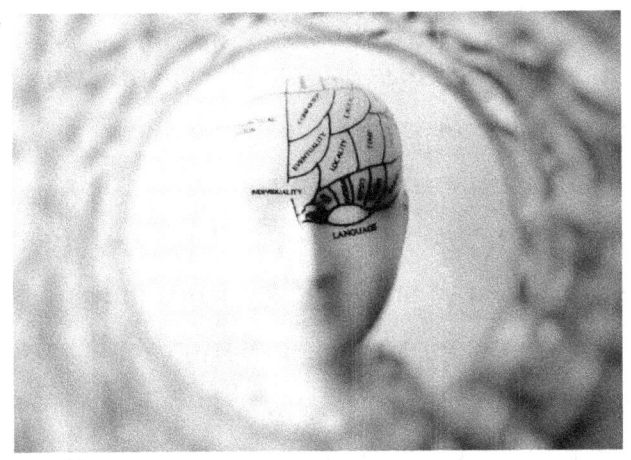

"I've a grand memory for forgetting."
-Robert Louis Stevenson

Can you recall the name of every elementary school teacher you had? Or are you the sort that gets all the way to work before realizing you left your lunch at home? Memory is a funny thing, and we tend to categorize ourselves as either having a good memory or a bad memory. That's an oversimplified view of a cerebral function that has many forms and many purposes.

Some people are exceptional at remembering names and faces, and some people have thousands of song lyrics imprinted in their minds. Some people would, as they say, forget their head if it wasn't attached, and some people are the proverbial steel trap. Which are you, and which do you strive to be? Before you begin making your 'memory goals', let's take a look at how the brain is constructed, how memories are formed and where the brain stores them for recall.

Overview of the Brain

The human brain is made up of four main segments; the cerebrum, the cerebellum, the medulla, and the pons. Each segment has smaller areas which have very specific tasks, and all the parts work together to make the brain function properly.

The cerebrum is the largest, uppermost part of the brain, and is split into left and right hemispheres. Each hemisphere has four lobes: the parietal lobe, which governs spatial orientation; the frontal lobe, which is responsible for decision-making and judgement; the temporal lobe, which processes hearing, language, and memory; and the occipital lobe, which takes care of visual processing.

The cerebellum is underneath the cerebellum and sits on top of the brain stem at the origin of the spinal column. The cerebellum's main function is to regulate equilibrium and muscle coordination.

The pons is a messenger. It handles communication between the cerebellum, the cerebrum, and transmits information down the spinal cord. Lastly, the medulla controls involuntary actions like heartbeat and breathing.

Each of the four main components of the brain are intertwined with smaller components that all have a specific function. The pituitary gland governs endocrine function, while the amygdala processes involuntary emotions. We're going to focus on the hippocampus, which is located deep inside the temporal lobe of the cerebrum. The hippocampus plays a vital role in the storage of long-term memories. By discovering how this vital brain component functions, you'll be able to see why it's so crucial in the learning process. In the graphic below, you'll see the mains parts of the brain marked out according to their functions. Each section is highly specialized to perform certain tasks which make up the whole of the human brain's activity.

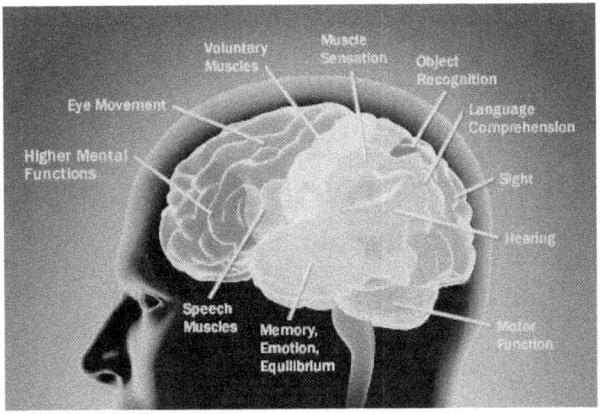

The Brain, Sorted by Function

The Hippocampus

The hippocampus, as we've just learned, is the part of the brain which governs long-term memory. It is divided into two halves, with each half sitting on one side of the line between the hemispheres of the brain. This small portion of the organ is responsible for forming and storing long-term memories, mentally cataloging new surroundings, and filing away statistical facts, likes names and numbers.

Damage to the hippocampus can cause memory loss, and patients with Alzheimer's disease show significant loss of function in the hippocampus. As part of the body's limbic system, the hippocampus also aids with spatial awareness and emotional responses.

When the hippocampus is functioning properly, it's the area of the brain where long-term memories are stored. Short-term memories are not a function of the hippocampus; the cerebral cortex and cerebellum handle those memories, as well as handling procedural memories, such as walking or running. The hippocampus also does not seem to be involved in the process of learning a new skill.

There are two types of memory loss which can occur with traumatic damage to the hippocampus. Retrograde amnesia means the temporary or permanent loss of long-term memories. Anterograde amnesia is the inability to form or store any new memories.

The Hippocampus Uses Filing Cabinets

The hippocampus itself is made up of three segments, which are almost like file cabinets. The dorsal hippocampus stores spatial information, as well as verbal and conceptual memories. The ventral hippocampus files away conditioned behaviors and fear responses. The intermediate hippocampus functions as a go-between and manages overflow from the dorsal and ventral sections. That is to say, the intermediate hippocampus displays characteristics of the other two parts, and seems to exist to be able to function in either manner.

How Does the Filing System Work?

The functions of the brain have been studied for decades and while neuroscientists are still trying to figure out everything the brain does and everything it can do, researchers have known for many years that the hippocampus is a long-term storage facility.

The hippocampus stores experiential memories by taking data from the brain's processing centers, like the frontal cortex, and encoding that data as 'autobiographical'. The hippocampus is where your brain stores things like your early childhood memories, your first crush, or mental images of your first car. The hippocampus relies heavily on the sensory information it receives to determine if a long-term memory is, in essence, worth creating.

In relation to those long-term memories, there's strong evidence to suggest that the hippocampus takes emotional information from the amygdala and stores it as emotional memories. This is one of the reasons that strong memories have the ability to evoke the same emotional reaction as the day the memory was imprinted. These emotional memories could be triggered by something like hearing your wedding song, or visiting an important place from your childhood.

The hippocampus also specifically stores spatial memories that it encodes from the processing centers of the brain, such as the medial cortex. These spatial memories can be of the layout of a specific location, or navigational memories. Cab drivers have been shown to have increased activity in the areas of the hippocampus that store spatial memories, possibly due to the constant reinforcement of regular routes and the subsequent memorization of those routes.

It's the loss of the spatial memories in the hippocampus which is often associated with dementia and Alzheimer's. The damage to the hippocampus linked with those diseases can lead to disorientation and confusion. Injury or traumatic damage can also cause the loss of spatial memories.

What Else Can Affect the Hippocampus?

Injury and dementia-type diseases are not the only issues that can negatively affect the hippocampus's ability to create and store long-term memories. Studies show that post-traumatic stress disorder (PTSD) and mental illnesses such as schizophrenia and severe clinical depression can cause an atrophy of the hippocampus. Such an atrophy can cause a loss of recall of long-term memory, an inability to form and store new memories, memory distortion, and cognitive problems.

Stress and the so-called 'stress hormone' cortisol can also affect how the hippocampus stores and forms memories. High cortisol levels are also associated with endocrine disorders such as Cushing's syndrome. In many of these cases, lost hippocampal function can be partially or fully restored through pharmaceutical treatment of the underlying condition(s).

Epilepsy can also cause damage to the hippocampus and prompt loss of memory. The brain cells which misfire and cause epileptic seizures often suffer from hyperexcitability which can lead to cell death. Ischemic strokes can have a similar effect. Both epilepsy and strokes, as well as loss of blood flow to the brain have been linked to transient global amnesia, a sudden total loss of memory. Diagnostic imaging of patients with TGA often show small lesions on the hippocampus after the event. TGA often reverses course as suddenly as it occurs, with little or no permanent damage to the hippocampus.

The Inner Workings of Short-term Memory

When an event, a fact, or a mental image isn't deemed worthy of going into long-term storage, that doesn't mean it isn't a necessary piece of information. We use our short-term memory every day- to remember a phone member as we dial it, to order lunch for our coworkers, or to recall a dollar amount to write out a check at the mechanic.

Short-term memory has a very small retention window, about 20-30 seconds total. It also only has the capacity to store about seven items, like the digits of a phone number or a short shopping list. The brain only keeps those items on deck while we need them, and then the memory flees. It's only when we consistently use those items that they become committed to long-term memory. Before the advent of cellular phones, which store all our contact information for us, this might be a number you dialed frequently or an address to which you often wrote.

Short-term memory is based in synaptic function. As the brain takes in and processes stimuli, it creates a synaptic response. As the neurons and axons fire, the data moves down the line of cells until it essentially fizzles out. The brief duration can be reset by reading or reciting the information again. Memory 'chunking' can also help restart the clock on a short-term memory. This entails breaking down the needed information into smaller pieces of data.

The most common example of chunking is a standard ten-digit phone number. Observe this string of numbers:

9735551234

And this one:

973-555-1234

By breaking the digits into groups, the brain can more easily interpret and recall the data as a whole. Other examples of this might be trying to memorize a social security number or account information.

The graph shown below is known as an Ebbinghaus Memory Curve, or 'forgetting curve'. It shows the speed at which a short-term memory is lost, and how the recall of information levels off over time. The chart, which was developed by German psychologist Hermann Ebbinghaus in the mid-1880s, does not account for any additional rehearsal of information- simply a piece of data given once and then tested for recall over the specified time period. Rehearsal or practice is typically accounted for and depicted by a learning curve, also developed by Ebbinghaus. He also conducted pioneering research on learning, leaning heavily on the theory of spaced repetition and using mnemonic devices.

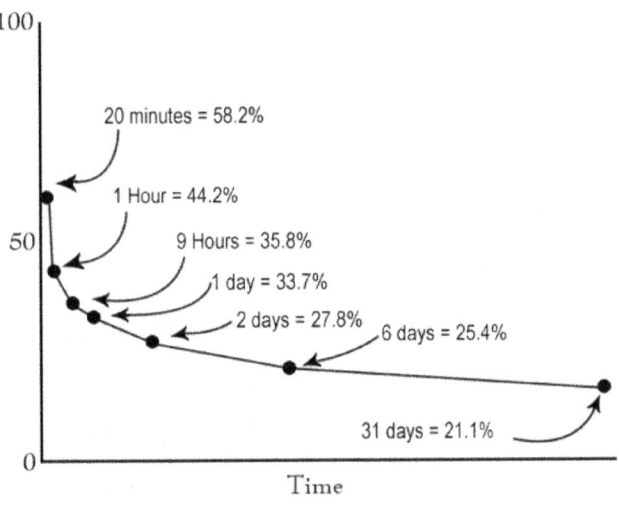

Ebbinghaus Memory Curve

What About Working Memory?

Somewhere between the fleeting nature of short-term memory and the staying power of long-term memory is the middle ground of working memory. Working memory is a cocktail of sorts, part new information, part stored data, part cognitive function, and part rapid processing.

When we refer to working memory, an example might be completing a new task at work. You're familiar with your company's policies and procedures, and you know that based on that knowledge, you can complete the new work- that's your long-term memory. You are also processing information pertinent to the new task- perhaps a new software program that needs to be learned on the fly to meet a deadline, and you've committed the password to that program to your short-term memory.

Now, imagine your feelings on Day 1 of the new project. You're feeling a little nervous, you're trying to take in a lot of information at once, and you're trying to calm down and rely on your experience. Jump to Day 5. You've begun to get the hang of it, and you're handling the task with much more ease. You've acclimated to the software, and you've gotten to know the data a little better. All the things that were thrown at you on the first day have started to become familiar. You've built a working memory.

The question now becomes, will that working memory become a long-term memory? That's up to the cortex and the hippocampus. If the frontal cortex determines from the available data that the task you've been training in is a one-time deal, the process may not be committed to the hippocampus. If the work is something that is becoming part of your everyday job going forward, or is something you'll be asked to complete regularly, it will be filed away as a long-term memory.

Practice and repetition are the keys to the evolution of a memory from short-term to working to long-term. In the next chapter, we'll delve into the hows and whys of practice and studying, and how best to apply your efforts to make maximum strides in your learning goals.

CHAPTER 5
THE IMPORTANCE OF PRACTICE - Using Study and Hard Work to Produce Gratifying Results

"The reason a lot of people do not recognize opportunity is because it usually goes around wearing overalls looking like hard work."
- Thomas Alva Edison

When it comes to any learning goal, it would be remiss to underestimate the power of hard work and effective study habits. Everyone's brain is wired differently, and we've already briefly covered different learning styles. What may come easily to one person takes a lot of perseverance and study for another person to learn. Innate intelligence plays a role into the pace and effectiveness of learning, as well. Let's take a more detailed look at methods of study and how to use them to your learning advantage.

Be S.M.A.R.T. About Your Goals

Knowing what you want to accomplish when committing yourself to the learning process is a crucial first step. It's important to set goals that you can feel good about and that will take you on a direct path to achievement. The S.M.A.R.T. system can give you a template for determining the best way to get from Point A to Point B by teaching you to consider all aspects of your learning objectives. S.M.A.R.T is an acronym for Specific, Measurable, Achievable, Relevant, Time-Bound. By writing out your goals according to this system, you can hold yourself accountable to what you want to accomplish.

The S.M.A.R.T. system was first developed in the late 1970s and early 1980s by a business consultant and corporate planner named George T. Doran. Doran and others believed that large corporations could benefit from a goal-setting method that would function for all levels of business management.

Along with co-authors James Cunningham and Arthur Miller, Doran published an article in the November 1981 edition of the trade magazine, Management Review. In the nearly three decades since, the method has undergone little change due to its remarkable practicality. As the name would imply, making S.M.A.R.T. goals is a five-step process. Let's examine it piece by piece:

Specific- To get started, write down your goal. Sounds simple, right? But you want to be as detailed as possible. Write what you want to achieve. Then also write why you want to achieve it. Write down who, beyond yourself, will be involved in making your goal possible, whether it's finding a particular instructor or needing the support of a partner or your family. Then think about how you'll reach your goal. Will you need to rethink your schedule to take a class and/or have time to study? The more information you write down for this first step, the better to fill out the rest of the steps.

Measurable- How will you know if you are making any progress? This step is to help you determine what metrics are available to you to be able to judge where you are in your learning process. For some goals, this may be as easy as taking examinations or successfully carrying out a skill. For other goals, you may need to create a system to measure yourself against your past performances. If you have a tutor or mentor, you could ask them how best to make your goal a measurable one.

Achievable- Be realistic with yourself. Goal-setting is supposed to be a positive experience, so examine your objectives and make sure you've been specific enough to not set yourself up for failure. If the goal seems too large, go back to step one and break it down into some smaller pieces. While learning should push you to new limits, it should never break you along the way. Don't bite off more than you can chew; you'll only grow frustrated and hurt your learning process.

Relevant- This step is two-fold. Think about the benefits of your learning goal, and why it's important to you. Do you need to pick up a certification or complete continuing education credits for your job? Do you need to learn a new language for business or leisure travel?

Have you just always wanted to play the piano? Whatever your learning objective, make sure it's the right one for you *before* you get started. And once you do, make sure the information you're taking in is the most relevant, up-to-date learning material you can access. You don't want to get off-track by needing to go back and relearn things you've already spent time on.

Time-bound- The last step in the S.M.A.R.T. process is critical. You'll need to set a realistic timeframe in which to complete your goal. Deadlines are important to staying accountable to yourself and others. By setting a deadline, you're giving yourself not only something to work towards, but something to look forward to. The sense of accomplishment from completing a goal on or ahead of schedule plays right back into those endorphins we talked about earlier.

Writing your goal statement- Once you've worked through all your steps, you'll want to distill the whole process down into a clear, concise statement, like the example below:

"I will complete X course, working with Y instructor. We will use the ABC method, DEF workbook, and I'll take six online exams to measure my progress. I'd like to learn this subject because I want to advance in my career. I plan on taking and passing the certification test on December 15th of this year."

Your goal statement should answer every basic question: who, what, why, where, when, and how? If it doesn't, then you should go back through your previous steps to determine what's missing. If the method seems tedious, take heart. Like other things, it becomes easier with practice. You can also take comfort in knowing that by taking time and laying out your goals so specifically before you get started means less chance of wasting time by setting the wrong goal or getting off track later on.

A wonderful trait of the S.M.A.R.T. Goal system is that it works on any scale, and therefore it's a perfect place to start building your learning experience. Once you've got a solid goal or two set for yourself, it's time to think about the logistics of studying and practicing towards those goals. How you apply yourself to your studies will have a huge impact on how quickly you can reach your learning objectives.

Some Homework on How to Do Your Homework

When you were a younger learner, did you have an easier time doing your schoolwork in a quiet, calm space, or amidst the afterschool chaos of your family's kitchen? Some people need absolute peace to be able to learn, and some people thrive on background noise and distraction. The environment in which we learn is just as important to effective studying as knowing how we like to learn. Here are some key questions to ask yourself before you start studying anything:

- What type of learner am I?

- Do I need quiet, or do I need/want some background noise?

- What type of furnishings/equipment do I need to study my desired subject?

- Will I have access to the proper electronics and internet?

- What type of stationery supplies do I need and how will I access/store them?

- What will motivate me to complete my studying each day?

Use your answers to these questions to help set up a study space for yourself that will allow you to maximize your learning potential. Let's say you're a visual learner, who prefers to have a little noise to aid in concentration. Setting yourself up with a desk space for your computer and notebooks would be a good start. Getting yourself a radio or small TV for background noise would be helpful, or you can find a set of headphones to stream music or talk radio from a handheld device.

A visual learner would also want to have some good pens, pencils and highlighters for taking notes and marking important information. Index cards for making flashcards might be another supply to consider. As to the motivation, that's up to you. Perhaps you could set a minimum time goal for study per day, and set up a personal rewards system. Some people like to pay themselves a study allowance, to save towards a special item or experience.

It may be that the desire to learn is all the motivation you need, but we all have days where we don't feel like working. No matter where you set yourself up to study, write your goal statement down clearly and hang it up where you can see it, every single day. It will serve both as inspiration and a reminder of what you are working towards.

Let's Study Studying

Once you've determined your learning style and the best environment for you to study in, it's time to actually do some learning. There are some universal habits that make for highly effective study time, no matter your learning space or style.

Studying at the same time every day: This will train your brain to be open to studying. When you're consistent in your time and methods, you'll begin to learn faster and more efficiently. Plan which days of the week you're going to work on your studies, and study at the same time on each of those days.

Don't cram: Rome wasn't built in a day, and you cannot learn an entire textbook or course in one sitting. Even if you find yourself short on study time, it's still more effective to use chunking to retain larger lists of information in a smaller timeframe.

Order counts: Begin your study session with the most difficult tasks. Once you've worked through the tough stuff, the less challenging material will seem even easier. You'll also want to prioritize the material you need to know sooner.

Procrastinator? Just do it: You're tired. It was a long day at work. You just want to have dinner and watch TV. You can always study tomorrow. Don't procrastinate in your studying. If you fall into the procrastination trap, you'll fall out of good learning habits.

Don't consider it a chore: Adult learners usually have the luxury of choosing their subjects. However, if there comes a time as an adult learner that the subject matter isn't of your choosing, or turns out to be boring, try to see it as an opportunity and not a chore. Learning is a gift not to be squandered. You never know when you might use the knowledge you were 'forced' to learn.

Set specific goals: Each of your study sessions should have a purpose. Whether your aim is to get through a particular chapter or unit, make progress on a list of terms you need to memorize, or to tackle a set of math problems that needs to be worked through, make sure you know what you intend to accomplish at study time. Write these goals down if you need to reinforce them for yourself.

Get some rest: It's really hard to concentrate when you're tired. Be sure to get enough sleep and try to study when your mind is fresh and rested. Avoid studying with the false energy and alertness brought on by too much caffeine or sugar.

Avoid ennui and pigeonholing- Even if you're convinced that you can *only* learn through reading, or *only* learn through watching, switch it up every once in a while. Having your head tucked into a textbook all the time may also mean you could miss a learning opportunity dangling in front of you. Explore learning from different types of materials to avoid boredom and missed chances.

Stay positive: Even when you're struggling with a subject, don't let it discourage you. Focus on how much you've already learned, rather than worrying over what you *haven't* mastered yet. If you stop and think positively about it, you'll be amazed at how far you've already come in your studies.

Review. Then review it again: Remember that when taking the time to learn a new skill or subject, it's important to make sure you turn the knowledge into long-term memory. In order to do that, repetition and review are key. Make sure you review your notes regularly to encode the information onto your brain.

Below is a chart showing Ebbinghaus's learning curve which is almost the exact opposite of the forgetting curve. You'll see in the learning curve, the amount of times something is reviewed or practiced, the closer it gets to becoming 'learned', and the curve levels off.

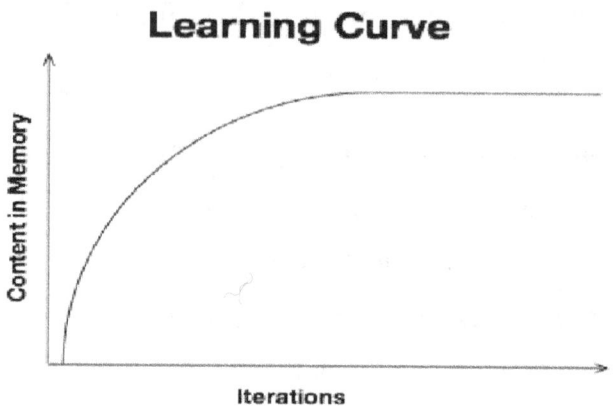

Ebbinghaus Learning Curve

Don't Discount Perseverance

Barring prodigies, not too many people can say that they have instantly mastered a new task or skill. It takes time, study, practice, and hard work to truly learn something, so do not get discouraged if you cannot immediately grasp a concept. If you commit to good study or practice habits, you will achieve your goals. Do not ever discount the value of hard work and perseverance. Let's go over some general guidelines for practicing new skills.

Practice, Practice, Practice

It's how, they say proverbially, you get to Carnegie Hall. Time spent building and utilizing practice skills will aid you in all types of learning situations, but for our purposes let's use taking up a new instrument as an example.

Imagine you've always wanted to play the saxophone. You look up music stores in your area, and find a prospective instructors. You purchase some beginner books and supplies, and rent yourself an instrument. You get to your first lesson, and halfway through, you're struggling to even hold the saxophone properly and you're not grasping the bare basics of music notation. Panic sets in! What were you thinking?!?!?!

Take a deep breath and relax. Go home from your lesson and begin considering your options. You could give up immediately. You could just show up for the lesson every week, wasting money and time and never improving. Or you could set your mind to the task and figure out how to reach your goals. Practice skills to the rescue! Where do you start?

Determine your goals: Set your end goal. We've already discussed goal-setting, so this should align with what you want your end skill to be. In this case, it's being proficient at playing the saxophone.

Break the goal into chunks: Turn your monumental task into easily handled segments. What do you need to learn to play the sax? You need to learn music notation and theory. You need to learn how to hold the instrument. You need to learn finger placement, patterns, and movement. You need to learn embouchure and breath control, as well as scales and simple songs. Only once you've mastered the basics, can you begin to move up in skill level.

Slow it down: Try practicing each skill slowly, then gradually work your way up to full speed. Taking time and deliberating over each motion or note change will help commit it to memory, for both your brain and your muscles.

Set aside dedicated practice time: Just like studying an academic skill, learning a physical task needs time devoted to practice. Determine how much time you can set aside every day or every week for practice time and make sure you stick to it. Make a list of what you want to accomplish in each practice session. Don't procrastinate or put it off!

Don't ignore the basics: Once you've begun to master the skill you're working on, don't forget the building blocks. Even professional musicians begin their practice sessions by warming up with scales and technique exercises. Professional athletes don't go out on the field without stretching, and martial arts masters still work on their forms. It's not uncommon to see experienced prima ballerinas in a class with small children, working on maintaining their basic skills.

Practice makes progress: The old saying, of course, is 'practice makes perfect', but perfection is a lofty, intimidating goal. Be kind to yourself by realizing that it's much better to recognize your own progress than to berate yourself for not achieving enough. If you are working hard, applying yourself, and doing your very best, you *will* see progress with each and every practice session.

While we were applying these practice tips to learning a musical instrument, they can be applied to just about any task you set your mind to learn. Combine good study habits and strong practice skills, and you'll be able to achieve any learning goal you've set your sights on. Now that we've got a how-to manual for study, practice, and goal-setting, let's examine some of the myths and methods you want to avoid.

CHAPTER 6
INEFFECTIVE TECHNIQUES AND LEARNING MYTHS-
How NOT to Train the Brain

"We must not be hampered by yesterday's myths in concentrating on today's needs."
- Harold S. Geneen

While there are lot of correct ways to train the brain, study and practice well, and commit to learning new skills, there are also a lot of myths and techniques that are ineffective, or worse, even harmful. It's important to stay the course and stick to your good study habits, so as not to fall into any of these bad habits or be taken in by myths.

The 10,000-Hour Rule

For many years, the 10,000-hour rule was used to determine expertise. The rule states that one must put 10,000 hours of study or practice into a skill to be considered a master. That's a lot of time- if you studied 24 hours a day, you'd have to study for nearly 417 days straight to become considered an expert. Given that humans need to eat, sleep, work, raise children, and take care of other personal business, how long would it feasibly take to get in 600,000 minutes of study time?

These days, that myth has been largely debunked. People learn at differing paces and putting a set number of study hours on any skill has become outdated. Yes, some certifications and professional qualifications still require a set number of hours on a task to be considered competent, but the old rule has mostly been abandoned.

More recently, experts have suggested it's better to get outside input to determine your own mastery. Find a mentor, tutor, or coach to help you gauge your competency on your chosen subject. Feedback can give you guidance on where you need to improve and what you can consider 'learned material', and shape the next phase of your learning experience.

Choosing Sides

Another myth that's been afloat for years is that of a person being strictly right- or left-brained, and that this was determined by dominant hand usage. This has lent credence to the theory that left-handed, right-brained people are more creative and artsy, and right-handed, left-brained people are more analytical. This theory is highly inaccurate.

The truth is, we all use both sides of our brains equally, so there is no need to categorize yourself based on a notion of using one side of the brain more effectively. Lefties- you can go ahead and learn some advanced math! Righties, go out and get yourself some art supplies!

The 10% Myth

Another tall tale about how we use our brains is the myth that says we only use about 10 percent of the capacity of our brains. Evidence now shows that humans, over the course of a day, use 100 percent of their brain matter, perhaps just not all at once. This means, unfortunately, that there's no superpowers to be had when the brain is fully unlocked, as some pop culture tropes would suggest. We'd be better off seeking out radioactive spiders and cosmic clouds to become superheroes.* Researchers now say that how we study has a greater effect on brain development than what we study. Remember, the brain is an ever evolving organ, and it is constantly firing and rewiring.

*Disclaimer- that was a comic book joke. Please don't expose yourself to dangerous substances or circumstances in the pursuit of superpowers!

Building a Pyramid

Just like there are abundant theories on how the Great Pyramids were built at Giza, no one is exactly sure where the Learning Pyramid theory arose. The Learning Pyramid theory states that a person retains information in percentages: 10 percent of things they've read, 20 percent of the things they've heard, 30 percent of the things they've seen, 50 percent of the things they've seen AND heard, 70 percent of the things they've said or written, and 90 percent of the things they have done or taught to others.

Frankly, this just isn't true, and you shouldn't base your study habits on the learning pyramid. Education experts say that this theory is total nonsense, and the percentage numbers themselves cannot be backed up with biology or neuroscience.

Intelligence is a Fixed Point

Intelligence, and how we perceive intelligence, plays a major factor in how we learn. Despite what we might have once thought, intelligence is NOT determined at birth. Yes, people can get smarter. Raw intelligence has been measured in IQ (intelligence quotient) since the first tests were introduced in the early part of the twentieth century. These tests are designed to measure not what you've learned, but what you have the capacity to learn.

There's been a move away from raw IQ scores recently because they don't tell the whole story of a person's capabilities, and recent studies prove that intelligence can actually be increased through study. For a long time, students were classified on their perceived intelligence levels, and many lower IQ students were treated as if they did not have the capacity to improve themselves. We now know this to be untrue.

The flip side of this is using high IQ to motivate students. It often backfires; when a student is praised for simply 'being smart', they don't believe that they need to study to learn. This often results in poor study habits and disappointing results when those same students get to institutions of higher learning. Those students may still be the smart kids, but the students who work hard are the ones who will achieve goals and be offered opportunities.

The middle ground here would seem to be to focus on small, attainable goals that all work toward the desired end result, and to not let others develop misconceptions based on your intelligence. Don't let yourself develop misconceptions about your own intelligence, either! Learn to praise yourself and others for the effort put into learning, not simply for IQ.

Going with Your Gut

Always go with your first answer! Remember that from middle school multiple choice tests? Actually, don't do that. While it was long believed that your brain would involuntarily spit out the needed information on the first try, that's not completely true. It takes critical thinking skills to go back and review your answers on an exam or quiz. There's no scientific evidence to suggest that your first answer is any more likely to be correct than an answer you come up with after second thoughts. That first gut-reaction answer isn't necessarily wrong, but if you can, analyze your answers to determine if they're correct.

While the above advice applies more to formal learning settings, it can be applied to adult learning or independent learning situations, too. Critical thinking is a key component in being a strong learner, and being able to critique yourself is a great way to gauge yourself against the standard. If you've got a mentor or tutor, they may also likely administer some form of testing to determine your progress, and therefore you'll want to keep your test-taking skills sharp.

One Thing at a Time?

The old standard was that learning methods had to be singular and focused to be effective. That's not quite true, and in fact, we learn much better when we mix up the routine. Inside our schools today, teachers are using multi-media approaches to learning, and as an adult learner, you can apply these concepts for yourself, too.

When you're studying, don't lock yourself into a routine so tight that you become bored and lose motivation. While it's important to reinforce your learning material, do so with a mix of reading, visual aids, and film. Try occasionally changing up your location- study outside on a nice day, or set up different backgrounds on your computer. Sometimes a change of pace is needed to reset your brain. Remember, one of the goals is to keep your mind active enough to maintain plasticity. No one wants to feel as if they've become stagnant.

Imitation is the Greatest Form of Flattery

While that may or may not be true, what certainly isn't true is that imitating or emulating the experts will help you learn faster. The people who know the most about the things you want to learn are great resources, but it took them plenty of study and hard work to get to where they are. Simply copying them will not gain you any true knowledge.

Instead, take a look at their body of work and use it as study material. Most advanced learners, like college professors or scientific professionals, are published in journals or have written books. There are experts in every field who regularly publish in trade magazines. Look at where they are sourcing their own material, find out what their path to knowledge was, and pick and choose the pieces that can help you advance in your own studies. The simple fact is that you, a beginner, cannot learn at the same rate as them, the experts, but this a matter of proficiency. We all need to learn at an appropriate pace and that pace is based on our own experiences.

How to Avoid the Myths and Make Friends with Time

In this discussion of the good, the bad, and the inaccurate of learning methods and study habits, we've touched upon the T-word, TIME, a few times. It's important to set aside time for studying and practice, but life has a way of piling up obligations. With limited periods available to study, how can that time be effectively managed? In the next chapter, we'll take a look at how to focus your efforts and maximize study time to reach your goals.

CHAPTER 7
THE POMODORO TECHNIQUE - How to Ignore Distractions to Better Manage Your Study Time

"It's not enough to be busy, so are the ants. The question is, what are we busy about?
    -Henry David Thoreau

What can a tomato teach us about time management? A lot, if you are using a tomato-shaped kitchen timer to help you study. The Pomodoro Technique is an internationally used method of keeping time and increasing productivity. It was developed by a college student named Francesco Cirillo in the late 1980s, and he named his technique for the timer he used while working in his dormitory, which was shaped like a pomodoro tomato.

It's Pretty Simple...and Pretty Effective

There are only a handful of steps to the Pomodoro Technique:

1- Choose a task

2- Set a timer for 25 minutes

3- Work, uninterrupted, until the timer sounds

4- Make a checkmark on a piece of paper (one 'pomodoro' cycle)

5- Take a 3-5 minute break

6- Repeat until you've got four pomodoro checkmarks

7- Take a 15-30 minute break, and start over

Proponents of the method say it improves productivity by reducing distractions. Life, of course, has a way of interrupting, especially in this digital age of instant communication. The Pomodoro Technique will help you handle distractions by prioritizing tasks and setting boundaries.

Broken Pomodoros

If you come up against a distraction, there are two ways to handle it. If there is an incoming call or email that simply cannot wait, end your pomodoro timer prematurely (no checkmark!) and attend to the interruption. Then when you're ready, reset the timer and try again.

If at all possible, try to tell the person interrupting you that you will get back to them in a little while and continue your current pomodoro cycle. Doing so will set a boundary with your colleagues or friends, showing that your work or study is important to you, but that you are not uncaring of their inquiries. A simple "I'll get back to you in a few" should suffice, but be sure to follow through on that promise. You don't want to sacrifice good communication, either.

Why Does It Work?

Giving yourself a task and a set period of time to complete it makes you focus, but because the time period is a manageable 25 minutes, it doesn't seem unconquerable or overextended. There's also that good old competition factor-can you beat the clock and complete your task? Can you resist the urge to look at your phone or your email?

The break portion of the pomodoro cycle is important, too. It gives you a moment to breathe and to reset your brain. Even if you didn't complete the first task, you can give yourself a checkmark for working uninterrupted and jump back in when it's time to restart the clock.

This time management method appeals to our human need to feel accomplished, teaches us about the time needed to perform certain tasks, and imparts the skill of working with the clock, not against it. When you've trained your brain to realize you *can* achieve tasks in a set timeframe, you'll eventually be able to determine how long a task will take *before* you begin. That knowledge will boost your productivity in study and your credibility at work.

Does It Work for Everyone?

The Pomodoro Technique is an easy-to-follow time management method, and has proven to be quite effective since its introduction. However, not all methods are right for every person. Critics of the system say the 25-minute timer can actually interrupt workflow and make it more difficult to complete tasks.

Other people think the system is too rigid, or have a hard time using it every day because of meetings or other obligations. The creator himself, Francesco Cirillo, says the time periods can be adjusted if necessary, but that

25 minutes just seems to be the sweet spot. Like any method of time management, it's up to you to give it a try and determine if it's right for you.

Now that we've gone over study and practice habits, delved into time management, talked about learning myths, and dug into the physiology of memory and brain function, let's look at some very specific learning methods to help you achieve your learning goals. Part II of this book is full of tips and techniques, with plenty of embedded exercises to get you and your brain in gear and on the path to new skills.

PART II

TECHNIQUES FOR LASTING LEARNING

CHAPTER 8:
SPEED READING - Picking Up the Pace for Faster Reading and Comprehension

"I took a speed reading course and read War and Peace *in twenty minutes. It involves Russia."*
— Woody Allen

Speed reading is a tool that, once learned, can be applied in almost any learning setting and plenty of real-life situations, too. The premise is simple- to train the brain to process the written word at a fast pace, allowing for quicker study and retention. Before we get to some exercises, let's go over the steps necessary to get started with speed reading.

It All Starts with Your Eyes

Assuming that you are reading this book in English, you are reading from left to right. Slowly read this sentence, taking note of how your eyes move as you go. Is it one fluid motion, or do you find your vision jumping around a bit? The first step to training your brain to speed read is training your eyes to run smoothly and quickly over the written word. The goal is to practice scanning until your eyes learn to move as fast as possible. By doing this, you'll be strengthening and building endurance in the muscles that control eye movement.

Eliminate Subvocalization

Subvocalization is the involuntary internal pronunciation of the words on a page. We transition to doing this when we first graduate from reading aloud to reading to ourselves as children. For example, when we are reading a novel, we tend to say the names of the characters in our heads as we read them. That's often why when we see a movie based on a book, we might get upset to hear a character's name pronounced differently than we'd imagined it.

Sometimes, when we are subvocalizing, our lips will move silently as we read. In order to take up speed reading, you'll need to discover how to completely eliminate subvocalization. It's the first, but also the highest hurdle, in learning to read quickly. Once you've figured it out, the rest of the steps should follow with more ease.

To avoid and eventually eliminate subvocalizing, we need to venture into the abstract. Start isolating words as you read them and deliberately try to understand them without having to pronounce them to yourself. That may sound a bit weird, but it will work after time. As your brain becomes more accustomed to seeing words without saying words, you'll be able to pick up the pace. It's going to take a couple hundred words to start getting used to not needing to 'hear' them in your head.

Figure Out Your Starting Point

The only way you'll be able to track your progress as a speed reader is by determining your base. Speed reading is most often measured in pages per minute. A good way to figure out your baseline speed is by choosing a standard size novel, like a paperback, and turning to the interior, making note of the page number. Start a timer for five minutes, and start reading. When the timer goes off, see how many pages you've read. The average reader will have finished just one page. A speed reader would have completed two or three. There are, of course, online resources to help you determine your base, as well.

Over the course of an entire book, a speed reader will consume the text in a quarter to a third of the time of an average reader. Spanning over a longer period of time, the amount of reading material taken in by a speed reader can exponentially dwarf that of the average reader. If you'd like to track your speed reading progress electronically, there are websites and applications which test and record your speed reading results over time. If not, you can simply retest yourself after you feel your regular study sessions have started to take hold.

It IS Polite to Point

Using a pointer, a pencil, or your index finger to follow text as you read is perfectly acceptable in speed reading. It may seem counterintuitive or even childish, but one of the primary concepts behind speed reading is to be consistent. Using a tool to run along the line of text will help you take in each word at a steady speed. Consistency is key to mastering the art of speed reading, so try to move your tool at a constant speed with a smooth motion. This takes a little practice, but if you start slow, you'll soon find your eyes coordinating with your pointer as second nature.

Stay in Control

Control is another founding principle of speed reading. In order to become a proficient speed reader, you'll need to learn to control your impulse to skip ahead to the 'important stuff' and cause yourself to backtrack. Backtracking costs time and comprehension. While not all words hold the same weight (more on that next), not all books are created of the same content, and require differing levels of attention.

A pedantic textbook is not going to go down as smoothly as a beach-read novel. It's important to remember that the two components of speed reading are **speed** and **reading**. The reading itself is the more vital part of the process, so be aware that you may not get the same numbers on that textbook than you will on that cheap paperback, because the material in the textbook has greater weight and requires more critical comprehension. What is crucial, though, is that you can control your speed relative to the book you are reading to maintain consistency. Think of it like a dog show, where the dogs are being judged against their breed standard, not against each other.

Don't Sweat the Small Stuff

The little words don't matter. Seriously, they really don't. When we read at an average pace, our brains already skip over the small words- the articles and prepositions, the ifs ands and buts. Those words don't contribute much to a sentence, and we don't need to read them. Observe the sentences below:

- Tim went to the supermarket for milk, eggs, and bread.

- Tim went supermarket milk eggs bread.

The first sentence is written out in proper sentence structure; it has a full subject, predicate, and all the appropriate connectors and punctuation. The second sentence is what the speed reading brain should see. It's not pretty, but the meaning is not unclear. The speed reader still knows what Tim did.

Training yourself to eliminate these words is not nearly as difficult as eliminating subvocalization. Just practice slowly as you deliberately skip over these words until your brain just doesn't see them anymore.

Scanning and Skimming Your Way to Success

Now we're back to the big P- practice, practice, practice. The only way to improve your speed reading skills is by using them. Take up reading large chunks of information as quickly as you can, then figure out if you learned anything. The more you scan and the more you skim, the more you will train your brain to take in the important information as you go. Be sure to test your progress either manually or through a website or phone application.

What's the Bigger Picture?

Speed reading is a wonderful skill, but if you're not sure why you're using it, you need to stop and consider what the ability means to you, personally. Will you be able to learn non-fiction data at a quicker pace, allowing you to study faster and complete learning goals? Do you want to read your way through the fiction section at your local library? Do you need to buzz through a backlogged pile of periodicals or trade journals?

Speed reading can open all those doors for you, and so much more. Below, you'll find some exercises to get you on your way to success.

Speed Reading Beginner's Exercises:

Training your eyes- Forget about reading at all for now. This exercise is designed to develop strength and control of the eyes and eye muscles.

1- Look straight ahead and focus on a point in front of you. Turn your head slowly to the left, but keep your eyes on the fixed point. Now turn your head to the right. Repeat five times, slowly.

2- Stop focusing on the fixed point. Now turn your head to the left, without moving your eyes, allowing your vision to stay in line with the direction of your head. Turn your head to the right, in the same manner. Repeat five times slowly.

3- Bring your head back to center, looking straight ahead again. Leaving your head still, move your eyes slowly to the left, and then to the right. Repeat slowly five times.

You'll begin to notice how the motion of your eyes is relative to the motion of your head. Practice these eye movements regularly, but continue to pick up speed. You want to focus on the way your eyes move when you keep your head stationary (step 3). That's the muscle memory you will need to effectively scan left to right as you speed read. Work on developing speed and consistency of movement.

Training your brain-

Subvocalization is the most difficult thing to eliminate when learning to speed read. If the isolation technique in the chapter text doesn't work for you, try this: listening to music while you read. By splitting your attention between the sound of the music and the words on the page, you'll begin concentrating less on what the words 'sound' like.

Getting to the reading part-

To actually get on the road to speed reading, you'll need know your base speed, calculated from the method found above in this chapter. Next, you'll want to pick a couple of books or articles with similar content or a comparable reading level. Try choosing two novels by the same author or two long-form pieces from the same magazine. Pick one to start with.

1- Take ten minutes to read, at your normal reading pace. You are reading for content, clarity, and comprehension.

2- Read the same content again, this time trying to read the same amount in six minutes. Concentrate on the words, not the content. Use a pointer or your index finger as a guide.

3- Take a breather, then do it again, this time in 5 minutes.

4- Do it again- but in 4 minutes.

5- Congrats! You've just completed your first speed drill!

6- Take out your second piece of reading material. Read it for ten minutes at your normal speed. When the ten minutes is up, see how much you've read and calculate your page per minute speed.

You should already be showing an improvement from your original baseline. Practice this fifteen-minute exercise every day to see a steady increase in your pages per minute. Signing up for a speed reading testing website is a great way to track your progress electronically. There are many to be found with a simple search.

One of the things we discussed in this chapter was how to determine the necessary words in a sentence. In the next chapter, we'll take a deeper look at selective learning to speed up the study process.

CHAPTER 9
SELECTIVE LEARNING - The Art of Discerning What Information Is Necessary

"The only thing that interferes with my learning is my education."
-Albert Einstein

There is a lot of information out there, to be found in books and periodicals, in blogs and newspapers, even on social media. We are constantly bombarded with facts and figures. We first need to determine what's true, and then distill the truth into what we need to actually digest. When it comes to taking on an academic goal, that type of selective learning can be a useful skill for deciding which information is necessary, and which data is filler.

Defining Selective Learning

The term 'selective learning' is a bit abstract, and has a different connotation among various scientific disciplines. For the purposes of this book, we'll use the definition widely used by neurologists and psychologists, which is "the ability to select items to learn among other items, utilizing working memory and metacognitive function." So what exactly does that mean?

To put it in simpler terms, selective learning means choosing which material you feel is more pertinent to your learning goal, through the use of prior experience and critical thinking. It's the mental equivalent of the age-old "what three items do you want with you on your deserted island?"

Imagine you're on your way to the store, and your list goes flying out your car window. If there were ten items on the list, how many will you remember to get once you get to the supermarket? If you were going to shop for items for dinner, chances are good you will remember what you had planned on making. Your brain subconsciously selectively learned your priority grocery items. But chances are also good that you completely forgot the sugar that you were going to restock the pantry with, because your brain decided it just wasn't that big a deal.

Purposefully Using Selective Learning

When faced with a large amount of learning material, how can you use selective learning to retain the key items and mentally set aside the items that are of lesser importance? Selective learning is closely related to selective attention and selective hearing, and knowing a little bit about those functions can help you get a better grasp on being purposeful in your selections.

Selective attention is a cognitive function by which the brain filters incoming stimuli. If you are in a room with a blaring TV, a small child playing loudly, and another person who is playing videos or games on a cell phone, selective attention allows you to focus on the television program you are trying to watch. If the child begins to cry, your brain will change its focus to their needs, and stop paying attention to the TV screen. The filters in our brains are there to prevent us from becoming hyper stimulated by an excess of sensory input.

We've all had a moment or two where we felt overwhelmed by too many things going on. Forcing yourself into focusing on just one thing can engage those filters and help us calm down. It's one of the reasons the '54321' grounding method works for people experiencing an anxiety attack. By looking around for specific items- five things they can see, four things they can feel, three things they can hear, two things they can smell, and one thing they really enjoy- they've reduced the stimulus overload and jumpstarted their mental filters.

Selective hearing is related to selective learning, too. While many a spouse have accused each other of selective hearing as 'only hearing what you want to hear', in truth, that's exactly what it is. It's sometimes called the cocktail party effect. Selective hearing means you can wade through a cacophony of audio stimuli and only hear the thing you are focused on. This could mean hearing conversation with one person in a busy restaurant, or being able to listen to the performer over the roar of the crowd at an arena concert.

"It's a special hearing aid. It filters out criticism and amplifies compliments."

The ability to use selective attention and selective hearing means that your brain is already geared towards selective learning. It's an extension of the fleeting nature of those functions. Selective learning is a more permanent function, because you want to be able to use it to commit knowledge and skills to your long-term memory. Below, you'll find some brief exercises for tapping into your selective learning potential.

Exercises for Selective Learning:

Creating priorities when studying- When you are reading or reviewing learning material, try making a list of key points (be succinct) rather than highlighting the text. Once you've finished your chapter or allotted reading, look at the list. Which points stand out the most? Which points seem less important after review?

The points that seem to have the most weight are likely the key items you need to learn. Your working memory and previous experience of the subject are what are prompting you to prioritize that information. Now you can go back and highlight the passages on those topics or make more extensive notes to help you commit the information to memory.

Learning to make effective lists- Everyone makes lists, and if they don't, they should.

Writing down lists helps us remember what we need to do, what we need from the store, or what we want to pack for a vacation. To use selective learning to make more effective lists, try this:

Before you write anything down, take some quiet time to think- really think- about what you're putting on the list. Think about what the 'big ticket' items are, the necessities, or the really crucial tasks. Then write your list. If you lost the list, could you write it from memory? If so, you've selectively learned the items that were your priority. You can test yourself with some sample list-making.

Selective learning in formal education- When it comes to classroom settings, it is often a great advantage to be proficient in selective hearing and selective attention. With that comes almost a forced sense of selective learning. What do you think is going to be on the final exam? You'll want to make sure you learn those things- because that's what the instructor extracted from the syllabus and deemed vital enough to examine you on.

If you pay attention to the key points made by the teacher, you'll be able to selectively learn the proper materials. All three selective functions are based in intuitive thinking, so take cues from the course material and the instructor to best determine what topics you should be focused on studying. You can always refer back to the exercise on creating priorities.

Now that we've discussed some general learning techniques, let's talk about memory again. The next few chapters will detail some very specific ways to improve your brain's memory skills, through techniques and exercises designed to get you thinking about learning and memorization in new ways.

CHAPTER 10
NAMES AND NUMBERS -
Tricks for Memorizing Everyday Things

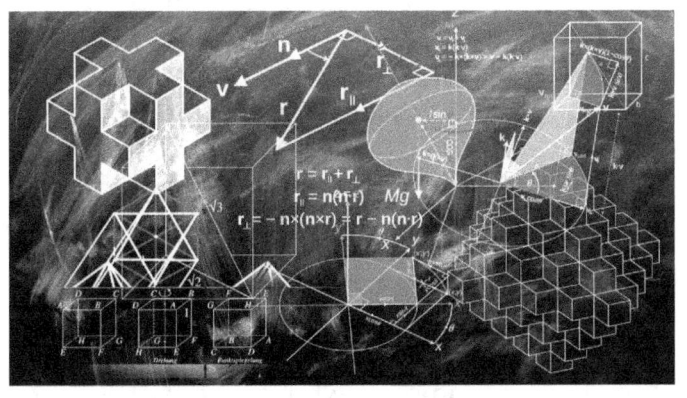

"If you wish to forget anything on the spot, make a note that this thing is to be remembered."
-Edgar Allen Poe

Ah, the short-term memory. It's a thing of fleeting beauty. It's what allows us to dial the phone without glancing back at a note, or count money and write the total down without recounting. But what about when you really need to commit facts, figures, names, and phone numbers to your long-term memory? There are methods to creating the neural pathways that will make your recall of everyday things more permanent. You'll find examples and exercises throughout this chapter that will help you choose the best memorization method for you.

You Know, That Guy...?

We all know someone who is 'bad with names'. Maybe it's you. It can cause awkward social and business interactions, and it's frustrating. You don't like hurting people's feelings, but you've tried and tried to remember the name of that tall guy from the accounting department that you speak to at least once a week, but you just can't. And what was your boss's wife's name again?

Don't despair. All it takes to improve at remembering names is a commitment to do so. Let's pretend you are going to a dinner party. You know you are going to be introduced to some unfamiliar people, so here's your chance to try out your new promise to improve your recall of names. Let's look at the few short steps it will take to reach your memory goal:

Make a mental commitment- Hold yourself accountable for your 'bad memory'. If you make a conscious decision that you are going to be better at remembering names, make sure you stick to it. Pep talk yourself about it before going into a situation where you are going to be meeting new people.

Concentration is key- You have to be mentally present to remember names. Don't just shake hands and move on. Observe what the person looks like, how their voice sounds, if they have a particular speech pattern or mannerism that makes them unique. Concentrate on taking in as much sensory information about them as you can during a brief introduction.

Repeat after them- When someone tells you their name, tactfully confirm it as if you hadn't heard it correctly.

New Person: "Hi, I'm Jonathan."

You: "I'm sorry, Jonathan, was it?"

New Person: "That's me!"

You: "Well, hi, Jonathan. It's nice to meet you!"

Within that short exchange, you've heard or used the name three times already, which is a great start to committing it to memory. Try to use their name during the course of conversation as much as possible without seeming contrived, and make sure to address them by their name directly when taking your leave. If you are at a business function, be sure to ask for their card, and once you have it, make a note of where you met them on the back.

Make associations- Think about the people in your town who are directly associated with their profession, hobby, or appearance. Every community has a 'Bob, the mechanic' or 'Susan, with the two little dogs'. We remember these names because we associate them with other things. If you can make a mental connection between someone's name and some other distinguishing feature, you will have a much easier time recalling their name with little prompting the next time you see them.

If you're a person who likes music, try to associate names with song lyrics. Or imagine an object or reference that resembles their name, like connecting someone named Shelby to the classic car, or someone named Tom to the old cat and mouse cartoons. The possibilities are endless. Be committed and be creative.

The Numbers Game

The human brain only has the capacity to hold about seven digits at a time in the short-term memory. That's why phone numbers are fairly easy to remember, and with repetitive dialing, they become encoded in the long-term memory. There are a few methods for memorizing numbers, it's up to you to decide which works best for you.

The Major System- This is by far the most widespread method of committing long strings of number to memory. It takes digits, which are difficult to remember, and converts them to letters, which are then formed into silly mental images and phrases that will jog your memory into recalling the numbers.

The system itself may seem cumbersome at first, but it can become second nature with practice. Here's how it works:

Using the chart below, assign the denoted letter sound to each digit you need to remember. Vowel sounds do not count for now, nor do the letters w, h, or y. You can use those letters to fill in the blanks to make words for yourself.

0 = soft c, s or z
1 = d, t
2 = n
3 = m
4 = r
5 = l
6 = ch, j or sh
7 = k
8 = f or v
9 = p

According to the key, the number 120 would become 'dnc'. Use your imagination to determine what that sounds like. For the purpose of this example, let's say 'dance'. Now, picture a miniature ballerina leaping up your arm. When you have the need to recall the number, bring up a mental image of the tiny dancer, and you'll remember 120 with ease.

This method is credited to Major Bartlomiej Beniowski, a Polish-Lithuanian military officer who went on to become an advisor to the Chartist rebellion in England. In later years, he published many books on a variety of subjects including mnemonics, and performed 'amazing feats of memory' in crowded concert halls. In truth, Beniowski's system was based on an earlier method developed by French professor Aime Paris, but the retired military man's popular appeal brought the method to the forefront.

Don't get frustrated, because the Major Method requires a lot of practice for proficiency, and it may not be right for everyone. But its longevity bears witness to its effectiveness when used properly, and that makes it worth exploring. If you need a time-tested, tried-and-true method for improving your number memory, this method has a great deal of long-term value.

Chunking- Chunking has been previously discussed, and so we won't belabor the point here. Just remember that chunking is extremely useful for everyday life. It can help you recall phone numbers, bank account numbers and PINS, credit card numbers, social security numbers, and so much more.

In this digital age, it seems that everything has a number attached. Chunking can be an effective way to commit to memory all of the crucial numbers in your life, especially ones that you'd like to keep secure. You can also use chunking to teach your address and phone number to your children, so that they can recite them to authorities if they get lost or separated from you.

The key to chunking is to break up information into pieces small enough to be memorized separately, and then put back together into a whole. You can also try attaching the chunks to a melody or sing-song, for easier recall.

Association- When you chunk a number and attach it to a melody, you're already practicing a form of association. The problem that the human brain has with memorizing numbers is that the digits often don't have intrinsic meaning. By giving the numerals a meaning or significance, you'll make them easier to remember. Perhaps you need a code for a bank PIN. Making it your own birthday isn't particularly secure, but how many people know your dog's birthday? If you use that, you'll remember it, because you love your dog enough to know its birthday.

This is effective even for longer numbers, like zip codes, dates of birth, or account numbers. Use anything you care about to give the numbers significance. Need to memorize a six-digit account code and love baseball? Try this- chunk the number into three sets of two. Look at the roster of your favorite baseball team and see which three players wear those numbers. Now you have a list of three names you can remember instead of six meaningless digits. For example, you love the New York Yankees, and you have to memorize an account number for work, which is 231502. Who are your favorite Yanks to wear those numbers? Now you can say, "Mattingly, Munson, Jeter" and you'll recall the number.

Patterns- The human brain can process patterns easier than it can random objects. If there's any way to create a pattern out of the numbers you need to memorize, you'll have an easier time committing the digits to memory. Again, here's where a sing-song tune may help you, or a rhythm to recite the numbers to. You could also look for repeated numbers and occurrences of symmetry to help you remember the digits.

Repetition- Like all memory exercises, repetition is a crucial component of memorizing digits. Try testing yourself. When you believe you've learned a new number, write it down three times. Wait an hour, and try again. Did you truly commit it to memory? If you didn't say it aloud, write it down a few more times, and repeat. When you can get it correct consistently hour after hour, you'll know it's been stored in your brain. Don't forget to practice it regularly if you need to.

Names and numbers make up a great deal of the information that we need to remember on a regular basis, and using the tips and tricks in this chapter will aid you in that task. Don't forget that practice and review are your greatest tools in the memorization of everyday items. A lot of the tricks in this chapter involved linear thinking and a bit of association. In the next section, we'll look at mind mapping, which takes making connections into the realm of the creative and the visual.

CHAPTER 11
MIND MAPPING - Using Visualization to Make Memorable Connections

"No memory is ever alone; it's at the end of a trail of memories, a dozen trails that each have their own associations."
-Louis L'Amour

In the last chapter, we discussed making associations to help you remember common information like names and numbers. Here, we'll delve into the more detailed practice of mind mapping, to help your recall of more complex facts, figures, people, and places. Mind mapping is a useful method for teaching yourself the connections between separate and seemingly disparate pieces of information. By using mind mapping, you'll be able to visualize meaningful connections between those bits of data and therefore be able to recall it with ease.

Drawing Bubbles and Conclusions

Mind-mapping requires that you've got some colored pencils or markers and paper handy. You'll want to start with a blank slate. Think about the main topic you want to brainstorm or learn about. Write that idea or concept smack-dab in the center of the paper. For example, you're studying the defining characteristics of a family of animals, let's say marsupials. Here's the center of your mind map:

Marsupials

Now, you can begin to map out from the center. Draw lines out from your center box. These will be your subcategories. Make one box for each marsupial you want to learn about: kangaroo, koala, opossum, water opossum. Leave room to add more sub-subcategories. Now, from each different animal, draw out to make boxes for each of the following topics: what they eat, where they live. Use colors to differentiate the categories.

Your finished mind map on marsupials should have a total of thirteen boxes, with the information organized from the center out. To further accentuate important points, make the lines connecting the boxes thicker or thinner depending on the priority of the data.

Below, you'll find a mind map template you can use to get started. Don't feel locked into this format, and remember to use color in your own mind map. Once you become more skilled in this learning technique, you'll begin to find your own style, with lots of color, shapes, and doodles. This technique is great for those with creative or abstract minds who have a difficult time processing information in a linear form. Remember, different points on a mind map may not only radiate outward, but may also connect to each other in other ways, too. That's okay! It means your brain is making all the connections it can, and you can determine which of the data or the connections is the most important, after the mind map is complete.

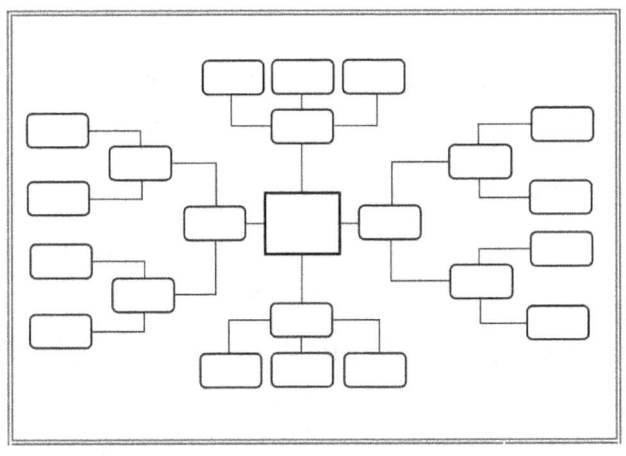

Mind Map Template

Why Do Mind Maps Work So Well?

Mind maps are effective learning and organizational tools because they work much in the way the brain itself does. The brain is constantly making connections and striving for plasticity. When you create a mind map, you are working *with* your brain, not against it. Mind mapping encompasses a more natural flow of information than data in a list form.

Mind mapping encourages both creative and critical thinking, and when you've made something yourself, you're more likely to remember it. Each line you draw and connection you discover is reinforcing the concepts you're mapping. By stretching yourself to make connections between the information, you're actively making new connections in your brain as you go. The more connections you can make, the more detailed you make your map, the more you will learn.

Using color and doodles will make your mind map interesting to you. People are always more likely to remember interesting things, so have fun with your mind maps. The bolder and brighter it is, the more it will stick with you. You can use mind maps for brainstorming projects, learning new information, memorizing facts, and creating outlines for written papers. In fact, you can use mind mapping for just about any endeavor that's going to require laying out, organizing, and prioritizing large amounts of information.

Those that mind map regularly say the method helps them be better, more efficient thinkers, and that they retain more of the information they've mapped. This is both because they have put the data into a memorable visual form, and because they've gone through the work of writing it themselves, which aids in forming stronger recall.

There are some for whom mind mapping does not work effectively, chiefly people who are strictly linear thinkers; they find the method to be distracting and too 'busy'. Despite that, most people like to give mind mapping a try, especially when it comes to outlining big projects. Another advantage to mind mapping is that it doesn't need to be a solo activity. It's useful in schools and workplaces to collaborate with classmates or colleagues for the brainstorming of (and task delegation on) group assignments.

Mind mapping is an exceptional tool for humans to work through and memorize information. But what if you could learn to use your memory like an elephant uses theirs?

CHAPTER 12
AN ELEPHANT NEVER FORGETS - Learn Like a Pachyderm for Better Retention

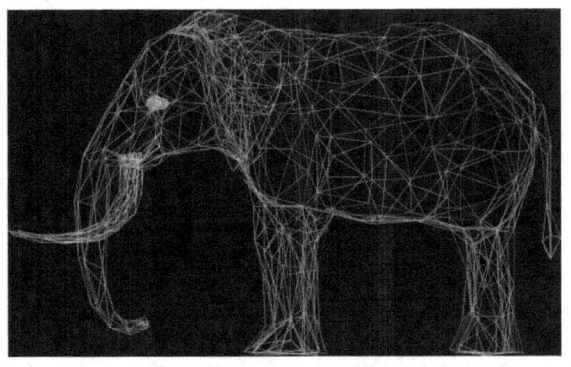

"You know... they say an elephant never forgets. What they don't tell you is, you never forget an elephant."
- Bill Murray, as Jack Corcoran in Larger Than Life (1996)

There probably aren't too many people who haven't heard of the legendary memory capacity of the mighty elephant. The earth's largest land mammals, these giant creatures have the brains to match, weighing an average of ten to eleven pounds. In the arena of intelligence, elephants measure up well against dolphins, humans, and apes, and are the only wild species known to recognize their own reflections in mirrors. So what's the key to their famously good memories? The answer is two-fold: survival and brain structure.

Remembering for the Good of the Herd

Elephants form matriarchal herds in the wild, and in general, the oldest female will be the leader, until such time as sickness or weakness forces her to step down. Because elephants are blessed with longevity, that female could be anywhere from 30 to 50 years of age, or even older. It's that matriarch's job to move the herd towards food and water and away from threats, and barring the ability to do that, protect the herd.

These matriarchs have to recognize each and every elephant within their own herd, and that could be upwards of 25-30 companions including calves which must be protected at all costs. Being able to recall the elephants in their herd also means knowing when another elephant *isn't*, and therefore could be a danger to the herd and its precious young. The matriarch will send out a signal for her herd to get into a defensive huddle with the babies in the center to protect them from intruders.

An elephant's memory for other elephants is so extensive, there have been documented cases of reunited animals recognizing each other after more than twenty years apart, despite only having been in the same circus for a few months. Experts say the extended lifespan of elephants is one of the reasons they've adapted to have such good memories. They need to be able to have long-term recall for the safety of the herd. Elephants also store the memories of their companions so well that have been shown to grieve for lost loved ones and, given the chance to come into contact with such items, will caress the tusks or bones of long-dead herd members.

Elephant matriarchs also have a tremendous working memory, which they convert to long-term memories for use to remember where food and water can be found in all circumstances. In one study of three herds over the course of an exceptionally dry season, the two herds led by older matriarchs were able to leave their home territory and travel to successfully find food and water elsewhere, while experiencing relatively low calf loss. The other herd, led by a younger female, stayed home and lost significantly more calves to dehydration and starvation. Why?

It turns out that the herds led by the older females had followed a similar migration pattern years earlier, during another extensive drought. Those matriarchs remembered where they had found resources the last time they'd been in similar conditions. The younger matriarch was not alive at the time of that previous drought, and therefore, did not know how to direct her herd to the alternate food and water sources.

Scientists suggest the size of an elephant's brain has a direct correlation to the breadth and depth of their memory. Elephants and other wild animals have their intelligence measured on a different scale than humans, using a system known as encephalization quotient (EQ). The EQ compares the size of an animal's brain against what scientists think the size of their brains should be, given the animal's overall body mass.

To offer an example, think about a peach and an apple. The fruits are about the same size and mass. A peach has one large pit in the center, and the apple has small seeds. If the fruits were animals, the peach would have the higher EQ and therefore be considered to be smarter. Elephants score fairly well in EQ, averaging just under 2 on the scale. For reference, apes and chimps are around a 2.5, and the human brain scores an EQ of approximately 7.

Because their brains are so large, elephants have a lot of cerebral space to process experiential memories. The hippocampus of the elephant brain is also large and well-developed to store long-term, spatial, and navigational memories. Their capability for retaining strong navigational memories are what helped those two herds through the drought.

Learning to Think Like an Elephant

The takeaway from the memory capacity of the elephant is that their working memory functions higher than that of most other species, and that's the quality which humans should strive for. How can you increase your working memory to make you a more efficient learner?

Working memory, as previously discussed, is the memory function most closely related to IQ. Therefore, in order to improve working memory, IQ must be improved. Remember, IQ or intelligence quotient, *is* the measurement of a human's capacity to learn. Now that we've distilled the equation down to the goal, how can you raise your IQ?

Experts say that brain games are one of the best ways to expand your IQ. Online brain trainers like Dual N-Back are great IQ boosters, and chess has proven itself to be a classic brain trainer. Other strategy games like Risk or even Connect 4 for younger children can train the brain to think critically and think ahead of itself. The reason these games are effective is because working memory is rooted in knowing the past, analyzing the present, and projecting the best-case scenario for the future. Brain games force you to consider more than once step ahead if you want to succeed.

Exercise is also a great way to expand your IQ. Cardio workouts increase the flow of oxygen to the brain. Exercise also produces endorphins, those feel-good compounds we discussed all the way back in Chapter 1, which will increase your capacity to learn. Meditation is also proven to help raise IQ in adults. Vigorous exercise and meditation also have a positive effect on neuroplasticity.

Like we talked about earlier, learning also begets learning. Some experts say that immersing yourself in a lot of different disciplines will help your brain start making cross-discipline connections, such as that between music and math. Try reading different genres of books, play games which might be out of your comfort zone, and take up diverse hobbies. The more things you learn, the more you will be capable of learning. Take the term 'renaissance man' (or 'woman', of course) to heart. You should strive to be curious about a variety of topics. It will do your brain a lot of good, and make you an interesting conversationalist on your next business trip.

In the next chapter, we'll spend time examining the form and function of mnemonic devices, and how you can create rhymes, sayings, and whole scenarios for remembering just about anything you need or want to memorize.

CHAPTER 13
MEMORY PALACE - Building a Mental Castle for Your Mnemonic Devices

"There are no rules of architecture for a castle in the clouds."
-Gilbert K. Chesterton

Mnemonic devices are, quite simply, tools which help us remember. They are based on the premise that the more meaningful something is, the easier it will be for us to remember. We are introduced to mnemonics as early as grade school, and those mnemonics can often be recalled well into late adulthood, meaning they have served their intended purpose. Here's a few examples you might remember from your school days:

Roy G. Biv- The imaginary fellow who reminds you of the colors of the rainbow: red, orange, yellow, green, blue, indigo, violet

Please excuse my dear Aunt Sally- The order of operations for basic linear algebra: parentheses, exponents, multiplication, division, addition, subtraction

Every good boy deserves fudge- In music theory classes, the notes on a treble clef: EGBDF

Anyone who went to a standard American elementary school might also recall:

In fourteen hundred and ninety-two,

Columbus sailed the ocean blue.

Mnemonics can take many forms; they can be acronyms, rhymes, nonsense sentences, physical tricks, and visualizations. Let's explore them in depth to see which methods can work best for you. We'll finish up with learning to build a memory palace- a mental castle where you can store your mnemonic devices for safe-keeping.

Acronyms and Acrostics

The first three examples listed above are called acrostics; these are sentences or phrases whose words begin with the same letter of the words that need to be memorized. Acrostics work as mnemonic devices because the sentences formed are almost always contrived and therefore, silly or nonsensical. Humorous things are easy to commit to memory because we like to feel good- remember those endorphins?

Another example of an acrostic mnemonics is:

My very educated mother just served us noodles- A fun sentence to remember the solar system: Mercury, Venus, Earth, Mars, Jupiter, Saturn, Uranus, Neptune. Of course, before Pluto's demotion, the mother served nine pizzas!

Acronyms are another strong mnemonic device. Acronyms are words that are made up of the first letter of each word you want to remember. The use of acronyms is popular in the naming of agencies and organizations. Originally meant to be a time saver, it's also become an easy way to remember what the organizations are and what they do. NASA would be an example of this in the American government. In learning, acronyms can help us remember important facts and figures. Here's a couple of examples:

Mr. MIMAL- The man who stands next to the Mississippi River in the Midwest, where Minnesota is his hat, Iowa his face, Missouri his torso, Arkansas his legs, and Louisiana his feet (MIMAL). Take a look, you'll find it really does resemble a man wearing a chef's hat.

HOMES- Useful acronym for recalling the Great Lakes: Huron, Ontario, Michigan, Erie, Superior.

You can use acronyms and acrostics to aid in the memorization of just about anything, and the best part is getting to create them. The more fun you're having, the more you will learn.

Feel the Rhythm, Feel the Rhyme

Rhymes are one of the first things we learn as a child, beginning with nursery rhymes and children's sing-songs. Many children's books rhyme, and Dr. Seuss tapped into the cognitive function of rhymes for preschoolers with dozens of classics like *The Cat in the Hat* and *Green Egg and Ham.*

Experts have since proven that adults also make a stronger cognitive connection to words and phrases when they rhyme, which is one of the reasons why some people can memorize song lyrics with such ease. But the neuroscience behind rhyme can be a useful tool to help up remember crucial facts. The ditty above about Columbus is one little poem, and here's some more examples:

Leaves of three, let it be!- Don't touch! It's poison ivy!

Red sun at night, sailor's delight; Red sun at morning, sailors, take warning! – To forecast the weather when ships were a primary source of transportation. Almanacs offer data suggesting this poem is accurate.

Thirty is hot, Twenty is nice, Ten is cool, Zero is ice- A little rhyme to help Fahrenheit users remember the comparable Celsius values. 30*C is about 85 degrees Fahrenheit, whereas

0 degrees Celsius is the equivalent of 32* F, the point at which water freezes into ice.

You don't need to use existing rhymes to use their mnemonic powers. Like with acronyms and acrostics, you can have some fun writing your own to make them all the more memorable.

You Put a Spell on Me

Spelling mnemonics are brief silly sentences which can help you remember how to spell some commonly misspelled words. Here are some examples, but it you have words you always struggle with, have fun making up your own!

Big elephants can always understand small elephants- To spell 'because'.

We hear with our ear- To remember which 'hear' (here) to use.

Never believe a lie- To remember the proper order of the 'ie' in believe.

'I' before 'E', except after 'C', or when it sounds like an 'A', as is neighbor and weigh- Of course, native English speakers will know there are many, many exceptions to this rule, but it's a good starter mnemonic for young schoolchildren.

Visualization Mnemonics

Some mnemonics rely on sight, rather than sound. These could be things as simple as imagining the number 8 as a snowman, or holding up your left hand to make an L. When we see things that make sense to the visual processing centers of the brain, we often have an 'aha!' moment, and begin to encode the image for permanent storage. Here are some more examples:

Making a fist to remember which months have 31 days- Ball your right hand into a fist with your knuckles facing you. Touching the knuckle of your index finger, say 'January', then the dip between that knuckle and the next is 'February', middle finger knuckle is 'March', next dip is 'April', ring finger knuckle is 'May', dip is 'June', pinky knuckle is 'July'. Go back to your index finger knuckle and start over with 'August', dip is 'September', middle finger knuckle is 'October', dip is 'November', ring finger knuckle is 'December'. All the months that fell on a knuckle have 31 days, the dips do not.

Using letters to determine species of camel- There are two types of camel, the single-humped Dromedary, and the double-humped Bactrian. To remember which variety is which, or identify which you are looking at, a capital B (for Bactrian) has two humps. A capital D (for Dromedary) has one hump.

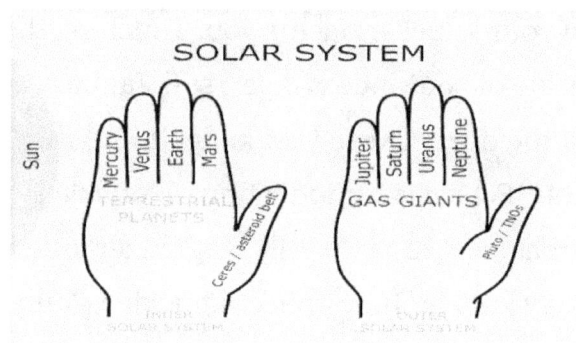

Solar System Hand Visual

Another solar system mnemonic- The graphic above shows how to use your hands to memorize the solar system, and is a bit more detailed than the planets acrostic.

Visualization mnemonics are yet another fun device that you can create with. Try to come up with the cleverest images or the neatest tricks to help you remember things better. Draw your own little doodles when you're studying or make little sketches to hang in your work area.

Building a Palace for Your Mnemonics

One of the best ways to use mnemonic devices is to create a world for them to live in. Some people call this a memory palace, or a memory castle, or you could use the fancier name 'the method of loci'. It works like this: You have a certain large amount of information you need to memorize or data you must remember sequentially. How can you efficiently and effectively store it so you can present it back properly? For our example, we'll say you are preparing an important speech for work, and it needs to be memorized. Let's get started!

Choose a location for your memory palace- This should be somewhere you are very familiar with; someplace like your home, your parents' home, your place of work, etc. You need to choose somewhere you know the way around and where you feel comfortable. You'll need to be able to see this place when you close your eyes. Design a route through that location- you can come in the front door, maybe go around the house, or to the living room. Make it a route that makes sense, perhaps like your routine when you get home from work or school. If you can't think of a good path, just focus on going clockwise through the rooms.

Choose standout features along your route- If you are tracing the route you take when you get home, you can start with your front door. Note other important features as you do your walkthrough. The table where you set your keys and bag could be your next stop. Onto the bedroom to kick off your shoes could be stop number three. Then you can go into the powder room to wash your face and hands. Next, head to the kitchen to make a snack, and lastly, go sit on the sofa in the living room. You've now marked six fixed points on your memory palace route. Jot them down somewhere. These are going to be the locations where you store your memories.

Encode the route- This is the step where you're going to commit the palace and the route to memory before adding the information you're going to store. If you can, physically walk the route, stopping in all the fixed points for long enough to really study them and remember their features. Do mental run-throughs until you've got the entire memory palace memorized and can comfortably recall all the details of your fixed points.

Time to make associations- Now that your palace is built, you can add the information you need to have live there. Since we are using the example of memorizing a business speech, let's attach the parts of your talk to the places in your home and what they stand for:

Front door- This will signify the introduction to the speech, which you can associate with opening the door.

Entry table- This will signify the purpose of the speech as you settle on stage, which you associate with setting down your belongings.

Bedroom- This will signify that you're comfortable on the stage now, and about to start the meat of the speech, which you will associate with taking off your shoes.

Bathroom- This will signify that you're beginning to clean up the loose ends in your speech, which you will associate with washing your face and hands.

Kitchen- This will signify your closing thoughts, and offering acknowledgements, which you will associate with getting a little snack to close your day.

Living room sofa- This will signify the conclusion of your speech, where you can take a deep breath and relax, which you'll associate with putting your feet up for some TV time.

As you begin to attach the text of your speech to the places in your memory palace, make it exaggerated. Picture your speech introduction as you enter the grandest castle doors. Pretend your entry table can talk and recites the mission statement of your speech to you. When you get to your bedroom and take your shoes off, have them run themselves to the closet and jump in while singing your speech to you.

You get the idea. The more ridiculous the association you make, the better the chance you have of remembering it. Visit your palace early and often as you create your associations. You'll have the pieces of your speech memorized in no time, and be able to recall the walkthrough the palace with ease when it's time to deliver your talk.

There are so many different ways to use mnemonics, you'd be hard pressed to find a method that doesn't aid you, even in some small way, to improve your memory and your study skills. In the last chapter, we'll discuss how to take all the techniques you've learned and apply them for maximum return, not only just while studying, but also while at work and at leisure.

CHAPTER 14
80/20 - Using the Pareto Principle to Maximize Your Learning Efforts

"All growth depends upon activity. There is no development physically or intellectually without effort, and effort means work."
-Calvin Coolidge

The Pareto Principle is a mathematical observation, not an absolute number, but it has been used worldwide to understand industry, economics, education, research and development techniques; the list is endless.

What the principle says in its most basic form is this:

> Life doesn't fall into equal distribution.

What does this mean for our purposes? It means that in order to effectively learn, you must focus your efforts on the correct methods and study habits to gain the results you want. The 80/20 part of the Pareto Principle, for the sake of our subject matter, means this:

> 20 percent of the work results in 80 percent of the achievement.

Let's break down how that will affect how you should study. First, the 20 percent and 80 percent we are talking about don't have to equal 100 percent. For example, if a factory has 100 workers, and only 20 of them do any actual work, then 20 percent of the workforce produces 100 percent of the labor. The numbers in the Pareto Principle aren't rigid.

It's not set in stone, just a guideline to show that effort and result are not always distributed evenly.

Use Your New Techniques

Going by the Pareto Principle, how can you find a way to maximize your learning production? It comes down to focusing your energies on learning how to work effectively. If 20 percent of your study time is going to produce 80 percent of your results, then you need that 20 percent to be the most effective study time you can make it.

You can use a lot of the techniques that you've learned in this book to make this happen. The Pomodoro Technique can assist you in time management. The goal-setting, study, and practice skills found in Chapter 5 can help you maximize the efficiency of your learning time. How are you progressing with your speed reading? That skill can help you get the most out of your study time, as well.

This book was designed to give you the tools you need to learn faster and more efficiently. The Pareto Principle was designed by an economist, and economists are essentially professional observers of efficiency. Remember, the principle is not a law of nature- it doesn't always follow a set percentage. Instead, try to recognize that no matter what your input/output percentages seem to be, the underlying principle always holds true- that the minority of cause is responsible for the majority of effect. If you think of the principle in those terms, it might be easier to understand.

Applying the Pareto Principle Beyond Study Time

The subtitle of this book is 'How to Improve Yourself and Master Your Memory with

Advanced Learning Strategies'. We've done a lot of talking about learning strategies and not a lot of talking about how they can help you beyond academics or mastering your memory. We've not talked much about how you can 'improve yourself'.

The Pareto Principle is one way you can take what you've learned in this book, much of which *can* be used in a variety of situations, and apply it to *every* situation in your life. If you are aware of the cause and effect of your actions and interactions, you can make your life more efficient at home, at work, and at play. You can use the principle to train yourself to improve all areas of your life.

For example, it may be that you're a procrastinator at home. Perhaps you're not crazy about doing yard work, but you know it needs to get done. Apply the Pareto Principle to work smarter, not harder. But the problem is that your outdoor tools are disorganized, so it takes a long time to find them and use them, meaning you just avoid doing the work altogether. How can you use the principle in this situation? Start by setting a goal to clean up the tools.

Over the course of a summer, you may hypothetically spend twenty hours doing yard work. If it takes you two hours to clean up the tools, and eighteen hours to do the rest of the work for the entire season, but you *never* have to dig for the right tool again, then 10 percent of the work caused a 100 percent increase in production. (Remember, the total doesn't have to be 100 percent.)

Not to Be Repetitive, But Repetition is Key

You can take the example above and apply it to any scenario because the cause and effect truth of the principle will always hold. Use it to focus on work projects. Use it to make your workouts more efficient at the gym. Use it to help your kids get their homework and chores done. The more you apply the Pareto Principle, the easier it will become until it's second nature.

One of the recurring themes of this book has been 'repetition, review, reiterate'. That's because only by doing the same thing over and over again can we truly learn and commit what we've learned to memory. Adult learning is a different animal from childhood learning. We can begin to teach our children these methods and make life-long productive learners out of them. As adults, we may have some things to unlearn before we can learn anew.

What Have You Learned About Learning?

Perhaps you've got plenty of history of bad grades and bad study habits. In Chapter 1, we talked about setting that all in the past and opening your mind to learning. Everyone has the capacity to learn, no matter what their past academic career would suggest. To follow up on that concept, in Chapter 2, we discovered what makes learning so fun and why it makes us feel good. Endorphins make the world go 'round, it would seem. That, and an innate need for competition, of course.

In Chapter 3, we talked about the effect of diet on brain power. Maybe this is an area of your life where you've not ever had much control. With the number of foods and types of foods discussed in that chapter, you've now got a grasp on how to change your diet to change your brain, and maybe even change your physical health, too. Many of the 'brain foods' listed in Chapter 3 are also heart healthy, low calorie, and/or high fiber.

Chapter 4 was the neuroscience and brain physiology crash course. Now that you know more about the hippocampus than you ever thought you would, you can use that knowledge to be discerning about how you are committing things to memory. The brain is a fascinating organ, and scientists are using developing technologies to learn more about its functions at staggering pace.

In Chapter 5, setting goals, and learning how to study and practice were the main themes. Good study habits and strong practice skills cannot be discounted as crucial components to any learning goal. These skills will carry you beyond the classroom into the workplace, and lead you to success in your hobbies as well. Being disciplined in study will help you be disciplined in all aspects of your life.

When we got to Chapter 6, it was our 'how NOT to' section. We talked about common myths and misconceptions about learning, and how to avoid them. Knowing what pitfalls to avoid can make you more focused and a stronger student. Allowing yourself to fall into 'learning traps' can get your progress off track. You can take that knowledge and be a better student of life. Before entering into any new enterprise, take the time to research the pros and cons and debunk the myths surrounding it. You'll be pleasantly surprised at how much more discretion you'll use and how much more efficient you'll be at going about any task the right way.

In Chapter 7, we discussed time management, and it's plain to see why and how you can make good use of your time in any scenario. Be cognizant about productivity. Look for the time traps in your life- spending too much time playing on electronics, or being a dawdler about chores. Whether you choose to use the Pomodoro Technique or research other time management methods, you'll be well served to incorporate better time management skills into everything you do. In return, you'll have more time to do the things you love.

Part II of the book focused on detailed methods for learning and improving memory. Quick! What were they? No worries, no pop quiz here, but let's recap what we discussed. In Chapter 8, we went over the basics of speed reading. This technique is used all over the world by millions of people. It does take practice, but it can be worth it if your goal is to be able to take in as much information as possible. Even if you don't completely master the techniques, doing the exercises *will* improve your base reading speed and quicken your comprehension times. This will be useful in study, at work, and in leisure, where you'll be able to increase your intake of all your favorite authors.

Chapter 9 detailed the relationship between selective learning, selective attention, and selective hearing. This is a crucial bit of information, given the vast number of stimuli that surround us every day. We can find ourselves stressed out and overwhelmed by the speed at which things come at us, and being able to apply mental filters is tremendously beneficial. Plus, you can use what you've learned in this chapter to block out distractions in many real-life scenarios.

Now then, what was the title of Chapter 10? Oh, yes, that's it- Names and Numbers: Tricks to Memorize the Everyday Stuff. This chapter gave us no more excuses about being bad with names or forgetting a phone number. The techniques and tips found here are the building blocks of all the other memorization methods- chunking, association, visualization. Learning and practicing these techniques are the best way to move on to be proficient at some of the more advanced memorization methods.

Chapter 11 focused on the time-tested pen and paper technique of mind mapping. This is the adult coloring book of memory and learning. This method greatly appeals to people with creative minds, but everyone can use it. One of the most beautiful things about mind mapping is that it can be used for just about anything you want to study, learn, brainstorm, or create. It's a very flexible method for getting out of the box of linear thinking, and should be employed with great abandon. Use lots of color and designs and doodles to make it truly your own. Once you've mastered the basic concept, there's no wrong way to mind map.

The wise and mighty elephant was the subject of Chapter 12. The memory of the species is one of legend, and we discussed the reasons and the evidence why. The working and long-term memory of the elephant has proven itself to be extraordinary, and we can work to train our human brains to have increased memory storage and raise our IQs, all in the name of emulating the elephant.

The penultimate chapter, lucky number 13, is where you can reference information and examples of mnemonics. In fact, by calling Chapter 13 'lucky number 13', you've now got a mnemonic to remember which chapter is about mnemonics. See what just happened there? There's solid neuroscience behind why mnemonic devices work, and if you follow along with the concepts, you can create mental jumpstarts for yourself to remember just about anything. The sky's the limit.

We also talked about a memory palace in Chapter 13. This technique is labor-intensive the first few times, but it's worth it in the long run. A memory palace is another fun, flexible tool for learning and memorizing just about anything- things you've written, like our speech example, or things others have written, like a long-form poem. The best thing about memory palaces is that they are imaginary, which means you can build as many as you like without paying real estate taxes.

That leaves us here on Chapter 14, and it's almost time for you to be on your own to practice the Pareto Principle and start working on Pomodoros. Let this book be a guide to you as you set your learning goals. You can use the pages as a reference and as a jumping off point for you as you work to improve yourself and your memory. Remember to work hard, work smart, and utilize the skills found in these pages, and you'll be well on your way on your journey to LEARN FASTER.

CONCLUSION

Thank you again for choosing to read LEARN FASTER: *How to Improve Yourself and Master Your Memory with Advanced Learning Strategies.* The solutions for learning that are found within these pages are applicable to so many academic, life-skill, and real-life situations, and you'll be able to take what you've learned here into so many different arenas.

The strong takeaway from this book should be the ability to be a good student. The study skills and practice techniques here will serve you well in all areas of interest, and should be applied purposefully and often. This book can be used a reference tool whenever you need little refresher and the examples and exercises here can be utilized at any time. Remember that you should be practicing frequently for best results.

The key to learning is within you- only you know your motivation. But if you're willing to work hard and study smart, you'll see the payoff. There's a theme throughout the book of 'repeat, review, reiterate', and that's because only through committing to your practice skills can you truly master the techniques in this book.

It's important to remember that it's not all about numbers and facts and figures, but about being able to apply real learning techniques to all your endeavors. The true proof of learning is when you're able to use these methods without hesitation, to tackle any project or undertaking that comes your way.

One last 'thank you' and we'll see you next time!

HOW TO ANALYZE PEOPLE

How to Read and Influence People with the Ultimate Guide to Reading Body Language and Nonverbal Communication

Tony Brain

INTRODUCTION

There are plenty of advantages to being a people reader. For starters, you can understand a person's emotions/feelings more effectively and adapt your communication to accomplish the most positive outcome.

Imagine possessing the ability to decipher within a couple of meetings if a prospective date has it in him or her to be a supportive, compatible, and inspiring long-term partner. Imagine telling through a potential client's verbal and nonverbal clues if he or she will negotiate on your terms. Imagine being able to decode through a prospective buyer's clues if he or she is likely to buy from you. Is a business associate satisfied with your terms and conditions to go ahead with a deal? Is the salesperson trying to mislead you into buying or are they speaking the truth? Can you read people's reactions to steering the communication in a favorable direction?

This is the power of being able to analyze people's reactions. You can predetermine the outcomes of different communication styles and adapt to the one that suits the other person the most to accomplish a beneficial outcome.

Plenty of conflicts we experience in our daily lives are entrenched in our inability to read or analyze other people accurate. We fail to understand how they are thinking and feeling, which creates misunderstandings. Then again, our inherent insecurities are all rooted in what people think about us. Will my partner cherish my existence in their life? Does he or she value me? Does my manager appreciate my skills? These are the most inherent fears that we operate with. Once we learn to read people, these insecurities and uncertainties don't bog us down.

Knowing how to speed read people accurately is nothing short of a superpower or secret magic weapon. Imagine possessing the superpower to quickly read a person like a book. You will be eliminating tiresome guesswork from relationships and focus on communicating with a person that is most suitable for his or her thoughts, feelings, and personality.

When we learn to become more telepathic and master the knack of reading other people, we can use our cards in a manner that is beneficial for us. You don't have to develop the knack of being an FBI style investigator to analyze people or understand how they think and feel. All you need to do is watch out for verbal and nonverbal clues that the person is constantly giving out to know what they are thinking.

A person is consciously and subconsciously giving out plenty of clues about not just what they are currently thinking and feeling but also their overall personality, ideologies, values, attitude, preferences, and much more. You only have to be perceptive enough to tune in these clues at a subconscious level.

I recently read a piece about how the content you like on Facebook can help determine everything from your sexual preferences to gender to relationship status. Imagine, your social media likes determining your subconscious persona. There are plenty of clues everywhere; you just need to watch out for them.

Even when we don't realize, people are constantly giving away signals about how they are thinking and feeling. When you know exactly what to look for, your intuition, perceptiveness, and subconscious communication increase multi-fold. At times, you don't understand people because you aren't actively tuning in to these signals. People are nothing short of an enigma, and learning to watch out for the right clues allows you to put together the prices of a challenging puzzle.

Our knack for analyzing people influences the manner through which we interact with them. When you understand how a person processes information and emotions, the message can be delivered in a manner that is most beneficial for everyone involved.

According to research conducted by MIT, the other person's body language is an accurate giveaway about the outcomes of the negotiation 80 percent of the time. This implies that the person is offering clues about their inner feelings and thoughts involuntarily almost all the while.

An individual's overall personality is a sum total of several attributes, including beliefs, learned behavior, childhood experiences, gender roles, birth order, peer influence, genetics, environment, and others. All these factors are noticeable in the way people speak and conduct themselves.

While a layperson may view people itching their nose as a seemingly harmless or reflex gesture, a people analyzer will always seek deeper meaning in the action.

For instance, if a person has been confronted with facts where their lies have been called out and they start scratching their nose, he or she may most likely be lying. These gestures happen at such a subconscious level that the person isn't even aware that they are sending out these signals or making these gestures, which makes these verbal and non-clues almost impossible to fake. These gestures are directed by the subconscious mind and are more reflex actions than awareness driven behaviour.

Research has it that a person retains around 10 percent of the information imparted verbally, and 20 percent of visually communicated information. However, we remember around 80 percent of the information that is conveyed using a combination of both verbal and non-verbal communication methods. This also means that if you combine both verbal and non-verbal communication clues, your chances of being an effective and persuasive communicator will increase.

Body language along with other non-verbal clues is important when it comes to analyzing people. When a person's non-verbal clues match their verbal clues, it is a sign of confidence, authenticity, trustworthiness, and clarity. On the contrary, if there is a clear mismatch between a person's verbal and nonverbal clues, it can indicate mistrust, deceit, and lies. The person may not be telling the truth or maybe trying to hide something. The lack of non-verbal clues can be an indication that a person is not telling the truth or trying to contrive/manipulate his actions to conceal his or her true feelings and thoughts.

Chapter 1: Reading People Through Their Handwriting

"Calligraphy is an art form that uses ink and a brush to express the very souls of words on paper"
— Kaoru Akagawa

Every person's handwriting is known to be as unique as their personality. You can make an in-depth analysis of everything from their behavior to personality to the thought process. Graphology is the science of studying an individual's personality through how they write. Handwriting goes beyond putting a few characters on paper. It is about glimpsing into an individual's mind to decipher what they are thinking and how they are feeling based on their handwriting.

Here are some little-known secrets about speed reading a person through their handwriting.

Reading Letters of the Alphabet

How a person writes his or her letters offers a huge bank of information about their personality, subconscious thoughts, and behavioral characteristics. There are several ways of writing a single letter and every person has their own distinct way of constructing it.

For example, putting a dot on the lower case "I" is an indication of an independent-spirited personality, originality, and creative thinking. These folks are organized, meticulous, and focused on details. If the dot is represented by an entire circle, there are pretty good chances of the person being more childlike and thinking outside the box. How a person constructs their upper case "I" reveals a lot about how they perceive themselves. Does their "I" feature the same size as the other letters or is it bigger/smaller compared to other letters?

A person who constructs a large "I" is often egoistic, self-centered, overconfident, and even slightly cocky. If the "I" is the size of other letters or even smaller than other letters, the person is more self-assured, positive, and happy by disposition.

Similarly, how people write their lower case "t" offers important clues into their personality. If the "t" is crossed with a long line, it can be an indication of determination, energy, passion, zest, and enthusiasm. On the other hand, a brief line across the "t" reveals a lack of empathy, low interest, and determination. The person doesn't have very strong views about anything and is generally apathetic. If a person crosses their "t" really high, they possess an increased sense of self-worth and generally have ambitious objectives.

Similarly, people who cross their "t" low may suffer from low self-esteem, low confidence and lack of ambition. A person who narrows the loop in lower case "e" is likelier to be uncertain, suspicious, and doubtful of people. There is an amount of skepticism involved that prevents them from being trustful of people. These people tend to have a guarded, stoic, withdrawn, and reticent personality. A wider loop demonstrates a more inclusive and accepting personality. They are open to different experiences, ideas, and perspectives.

Next, if an individual writes their "o" to form a wide circle, they are most likely people who very articulate, expressive, and won't hesitate to share secrets with everyone. Their life is like an open book. On the contrary, a closed "o" reveals that the person has a more private personality and is reticent by nature.

Cursive Writing

Cursive writing gives us clues about people that we may otherwise miss through regular writing. It may offer us a more comprehensive and in-depth analysis of an individual's personality.

How does a person construct their lower case cursive "I?" If it has a narrow loop, the person is mostly feeling stressed, nervous, and anxiety. Again, a wider loop can be a sign that the individual doesn't believe in going by the rule book. There is a tendency to rewrite the rules. They are laidback, low on ambition, and easy-going.

Again, consider the way a person writes cursive "y" to gain more information about their personality. The length and breadth of the letter "y" can be extremely telling. A thinner and slimmer "y" can be an indication of a person who is more selective about their friend circle. On the other hand, a thicker "y" reveals a tendency to get along with different kinds of people. These are social beings who like surrounding themselves with plenty of friends.

A long "y" is an indication for travel, adventure, thrills, and adventures. On the other hand, a brief cursive "y" reflects a need to seek comfort in the familiar. They are most comfortable in their homes and other known territories. A more rounded "s" is a signal of wanting to keep their near and dear ones happy. They'll always want their loved ones to be positive and cheerful.

They will seldom get into confrontations and strive to maintain a more balanced personality. A more tapering "s" indicates a hard-working, curious, and hard-working personality. They are driven by ideas and concepts. Notice how cursive "s" broadens at the lower tip. This can be a strong indication of the person being dissatisfied with their job, interpersonal relationships, and or life in general. They may not pursue their heart's true desires.

Letter Size

This is a primary observation that is used for analyzing a person through their handwriting. Big letters reveal that the person is outgoing, affable, gregarious, and extrovert. They are more social by nature and operate with a mistaken sense of pride. There is a tendency to pretend to be something they aren't. On the contrary, tiny letters can indicate a timid, reticent, introvert, and shy personality. It can indicate deep concentration and diligence. Midsized letters mean that an individual is flexible, adjusting, adaptable, and self-assured.

Gaps Between Text

People who leave a little gap in between letters and words demonstrate a fear of leading a solitary life. These people always like to be surrounded by other folks and often fail to respect the privacy and personal space of other people. People who space out their words/letters are original thinkers and fiercely independent. For them, they place a high premium on freedom and independence. There is little tendency for being overwhelmed by other people's ideas, opinions, and values.

Letter Shapes

Look at the shape of an individual's letters while decoding their personality. If the writing is more rounded and in a looped manner, the person tends to be high on inventiveness and imagination! Pointed letters demonstrate that a person is more aggressive and intelligent. The person is analytical, rational, and a profound thinker. Similarly, if the letters of an alphabet are woven together, the individual is methodical, systematic, and orderly. They will rarely work or live in chaos.

Page Margin

If you thought it's only about writing, think again. Even the amount of space people leave near the edge of the margin determines their personality. Someone who leaves a big gap on the right side of the margin is known to be nervous and apprehensive about the future. People who write all over the page are known to have a mind full of ideas, concepts, and thoughts. They are itching to do several things at once and are constantly buzzing with ideas.

Slant Writing

Some people show a marked tendency for writing with a clear right or left slant while other people write impeccably straight letters. When a person's letters slant towards the right, he or she may be affable, easy-going, good-natured, and generally positive. These people are flexible, open to change, and always keen on building new social connections.

Similarly, people who write slanting letters that lean towards the left are mostly introverts who enjoy their time alone. They aren't very comfortable being in the spotlight and are happy to let others hog the limelight. Straight handwriting indicates rational, level-headed, and balanced thinking. The person is more even-tempered, grounded, and ambivalent.

There is a tiny pointer here to avoid reading people accurately. For left-handed people, the analysis is the opposite. When left-handed people have their letters slanting to the right, they are shy, introverted, and reserved. However, if their letters slant to the left, they may be outgoing, gregarious and social extroverts.

Writing Pressure

The intensity with which an individual writes is also an indicator of their personality. If the handwriting is too intense and full of pressure (there is indentation), the individual may be fiery, aggressive, obstinate, and volatile. They aren't very open to other people's ideas, beliefs, and opinions. There is a tendency to be rigid about their views.

On the contrary, if a person writes with little pressure or intensity, they are likely to be empathetic, sensitive, and considerate towards other people's needs. These people tend to be kind, enthusiastic, passionate, lively, and intense.

Signature

A person's signature reveals plenty about an individual's personality. If it isn't comprehensible, it is a sign that he or she doesn't share too many details about themselves. They fiercely guard their private space and are reticent by nature. On the contrary, a more conspicuous and legible signature is an indication of a self-assured, flexible, transparent, assured, confident, and satisfying personality. They are generally content with what they've accomplished and display a more positive outlook on life.

Some people scrawl their signature quickly, which can be an indication of them being impatient, restless, perpetually in a hurry, and desiring to do multiple things at one time. A carefully written and neatly-organized signature is an indication of the person being diligent, well-organized, and precision-oriented.

Signatures that finish in an upward stroke demonstrate a more confident, fun-loving, ambitious, and goal-oriented personality. These people thrive on challenges and aren't afraid of chasing these dreams. Similarly, signatures that finish with a downward stroke are an indication of a personality that is marked by low self-esteem, lack of self-confidence, low ambition, and a more inhibited personality. These folks are likelier to be bogged down by challenges and may not be too goal-oriented.

Stand Out Writing

If a particular piece of writing stands out from the other text, look at it carefully to understand an individual's personality.

For example, if the text is generally written in a more spread out and huge writing, with only some parts of the text stuck together, the person may most likely to be an uncertain, dishonest, or mistrustful individual, who is trying to conceal some important information.

Concluding

Though studying an individual's handwriting can offer you accurate insights about his or her personality, it isn't completely fool-proof. There are several other factors that are to be taken into consideration to analyze a person accurately. It has its own shortcomings and flaws. At times, people may write in a hurried manner, which can impact their writing. Similarly, the way people construct their resume or application letter may dramatically vary from the manner in which they may write a to-do list or love letter.

If you want an accurate reading of someone's personality, consider different personality analysis methods like reading verbal and non-verbal communication techniques. Various techniques may offer you a highly in-depth, insightful, precise, and comprehensive method of understanding a person's inherent personality.

Chapter 2: Uncovering Insights About Values

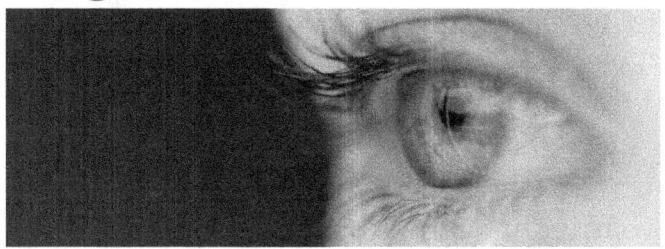

"Don't believe what your eyes are telling you. All they show is limitation. Look with your understanding."
— Richard Bach

Mind reading isn't about drinking some magic potion and developing telepathic powers overnight. It is a science that is carefully nurtured and mastered by people to attain success in their daily lives. Reading or analyzing people is a valuable skill that can come handy in any situation from approaching your manager for a raise to understanding a customer's needs to impressing a prospective date.

Here are some proven tips for deciphering people's values, wishes, and desires through their thoughts, behavior, and actions.

Watch for Hot Buttons

What are the emotional stimulants of a person you are studying? What is their comfort zone? Identifying people's emotional triggers is a great way of gaining insight into their beliefs, value system, and wishes.

A handy tip for learning more about a person's ideologies and values is to pose open-ended questions to them. Rather than asking closed-ended yes/no questions, pose queries that urge them to offer more in-depth responses. This can provide a glimpse into an individual's values.

Generational Differences

Though this is not a 100 percent foolproof method for analyzing a person's values, it can be an effective baseline for reading their personality through the manner in which they view the world. Generational differences may be more fascinating and insightful than people believe. Millennials focus on establishing more non-personal communication channels through social media or messenger.

On the other hand, Boomers may prefer face to face interactions where they can establish more meaningful and personal connections with others. They seek to set-up relationships where verbal and non-verbal signals are effective to make the most of their communication. Identifying an individual's generation can help to read them or try to establish a favorable rapport with them.

For example, if you want to close the deal with a youngish CEO, you know there are lower chances of them wanting to complete the formalities face to face. They may be people who are comfortable with technology and sending emails back and forth. Their value system or way of working may be more determined by technology than by the old-fashioned route of taking potential clients and business associates on elaborate lunches and dinners. Knowing a person's generation can help you gain insights into another person's values, beliefs, and principles.

Power and Authority

How a person handles power reveals a lot about their values, beliefs, and character. What is the individual's overall attitude towards people who they perceive to be lower in status? How do they treat servers, waiters, and other people who can't do much for them or who we perceive to be beneath us in the status quo?

Listen to them talk to a customer service personnel. How do they air their grievances? What is the person's overall outlook towards animals and children? The way people treat other people who can't return their favors says a lot about their values. Are they generally rude to individuals who aren't as powerful as them? Do they indulge in more magnanimous or selfless acts? This reveals an individual's real colors.

Individual's Contact List

It isn't a secret that a man is known for the company he keeps. One of the best ways for gaining insights into a person's value system and needs is through their friend circle. Are they with the same set of people for the last few years? Are they the leaders or followers within their social circle? Do they influence other people or are they influenced by the decisions and tastes of others? What are the types of people they dislike and like?

When you want to know more about someone's values, attitude, beliefs, and principles, ask them about the type of people they avoid. This is brilliant to know their ideologies. They will always avoid people whose values clash with theirs. For example, when people I pose this question to tell me that they avoid people who are high-handed or deceitful, it is evident that they are more drawn towards honest and down to earth folks. Similarly, a person who says he/she doesn't like to mingle with people who are always partying may be more focused, goal-oriented, and hard working. They are hard-working and want to achieve a lot in life.

If you notice carefully, you will identify a clear pattern in everyone they avoid. These traits reveal their own set of values. For example, sometimes you will notice that you just won't like certain people or you may subconscious avoid them. On closer scrutiny, you'll realize that they may all be ineffective listeners who do not show consideration for other people's thoughts, opinions, beliefs, and feelings.

They may be more focused on being heard and putting their point across than listening to others. All this will help you realize that people who dislike or avoid such people may boast of a more empathetic personality that places a high premium on tuning in to other people's emotions.

Language

A person's beliefs, values, desires, and principles are to a large extent revealed by their words. According to psychologists, we tend to emphasize on adjectives than pronouns while speaking, which offers subconscious indications of our persona. A high number of personal pronouns demonstrate an egocentric, selfish, and self-centered personality. It can also be an indication of increased self-awareness, honesty, and integrity.

There are other things that determine an individual's personality. For example, if a person is using big words or fancy terms to expresses their point of view, he or she may possess a desire to be constantly accepted or validates by others. There is a strong tendency to fit in or impress others. The individual may have faced rejection during their childhood, which led them to develop low self-confidence, low self-esteem, and feeling of never being good enough.

On the other hand, people who use simpler words and phrases to express themselves are logical, self-assured, and rational people who are confident of their abilities. They don't seek acceptance or validation from others and are fairly firm in their decision making. People who use words such as "but", "except" and "without" are mostly honest and truthful people who won't hesitate to share details.

Notice how people who are mostly happy, positive, and content do not use "I" often. Similarly, usage of "he", "they" "she" etc. are more focused on others. They place the other person first in a relationship while their own needs are put on the backburner. Even the kind of humor and jokes a person shares can tell a lot about their values, character, personality, and attitude.

Don't we all love celebrities to engage in self-deprecating humor? Or for that matter anyone who cracks jokes about themselves! It is a sign of high confidence, self-assuredness, and self-esteem. These people are confident and secure enough to poke fun at themselves. They don't think or care much about the opinion other people hold of them, which makes them take potshots at themselves freely.

On the other hand, people who are quickly offended by jokes directed towards them may not have very high self-esteem or may be suffering from an inferiority complex. A deep-seated feeling of insecurity or an inferiority complex makes them easily offended by jokes directed towards them. Thus a person's approach to humor along with the language they use can offer plenty of insights into their value system.

Reaction to Criticism

How a person responds to criticism reveals plenty about their values. What is a person's reaction to facing criticism? Do they get defensive, angry, and foul-mouthed? Do they fly into a quick fit of rage? Do they accept their shortcomings with grace? People who handle criticism with graceful are more confident, self-assured, frank, and forthcoming! They aren't egoistic by nature and consciously work on their limitations.

On the contrary, people who don't take criticism too well may most likely be suffering from an inferiority complex, low self-esteem, and inflated ego issues. They may need constant validation and appreciation. In their eyes, they can seldom be wrong. These folks may suffer from a high sense of self-entitlement or a misplaced sense of self-importance. They tend to be egoistic, self-centered, and selfish by nature, which means you'll have to employ a lot of tact and diplomacy while dealing with these people.

How Do They Spend Their Money and Time?

Time and money are some of the most important resources of a person's life and the manner in which he or she utilizes these precious resources says a lot about their values. Do people spend a lot of time and money on building a solid long-term future for themselves of their loved ones? Do they focus on the acquisition of knowledge, learning, classes, skills, and education?

Do they utilize their free time for upgrading their skills or waste it on frivolous pursuits? What are their pursuits, interests, and hobbies? Don't scan people's expenses with a magnifying glass now. All you need to do is observe how people use their valuable

Gut Feeling

We can master all the people analyzing methods of the world and still rely on our gut feeling when it comes to reading people. If you have a specifically terrible feeling about someone and can't peg it to logical thought, it may be an instinctive or gut feeling.

If you think your intuition or gut feeling isn't rooted in a scientific process, think again. What is termed a scientific process is closely connected to the limbic brain. It is a reaction to subconscious clues that the conscious mind has missed. If you develop a feeling that something or someone isn't right, your gut feeling may be bang on.

A Person's Negative Reaction

How a person reacts to someone who refuses their request says a lot about them. Are they respectful and graceful in the face of rejection? Do they accept it graciously? Do they respond in a more violent, aggressive, and volatile manner? Do they respect people's wishes and boundaries? Does the person manipulate people into turning their no into a yes? How a person reacts to refusals can speak volumes about their values and character.

Chapter 3: Analyzing People Through Their Environment

"Joy in looking and comprehending is nature's most beautiful gift"
— Albert Einstein

An individual's immediate environment can speak a lot about their personality, thought process, behavioral traits, and values. Of course, this isn't a pop psychology quiz that pops on your social media timeline every now and then about your hairstyling preferences and nail paint colors determining your personality. These are solid, proven, and scientific methods for making an educated guess about people through their immediate environment or the manner in which they live. There are clear psychological concepts and principles based on which you can tell a lot about a person through their environment. Here are some fabulous tips for analyzing a person through their surroundings.

The Closet

The mess within your physical environment is indicative of the chaos in the mind. This isn't about judging people through their environment; it is about analyzing people through their thought-driven actions. It is reading a person through their thoughts, which eventually leads to the creation of the immediate environment.

A well-organized, efficient, and systematic work station or desk is indicative of clear thoughts, clarity of decisions, good time management skills, and a need to get things done. The person is more goal-driven and is driven by a desire to take up challenging tasks.

On the contrary, a messy, unclean, and disorganized desk can be an indication of a chaotic mind that is filled with nervous and anxious thoughts. These people may suffer from low self-esteem, low self-confidence, and other issues. It can also be observed that excessive cleanliness can be a sign of mental disorders like obsessive-compulsive disorder, and reveal a more nervous or anxious mind that is filled with uncertainties and low self-esteem. There is an obsessive need to keep spaces clean and organized, which reveals a sense of inadequacy and disorderliness in the mind. The person may be trying to compensate for something they believe they lack by keeping their surroundings extra clean.

What is the first thing you think when you see a disorderly work or home space? Again, this isn't about being judgmental but reading or analyzing people through their immediate environment and setting. A cluttered space is often an indication of a cluttered mind. It can also mean that the person is a multi-tasker, who is keen on getting several things at a time. People who are busy or engaged in multiple activities seldom have the time or energy to organize their workspace. As a result, it is left unattended or in complete disarray. At times, a disorganized space can signal a plain lazy personality that reveals a lack of goals and clarity in life.

Again, you'd need to know more y digging a little deep rather than making sweeping judgments based on the space alone. It has been noticed that folks with a gregarious and social personality thrive in chaos around them. Peek into their drawers and they are most likely kept in a disorganized and predictably messy manner. They aren't inward driven or believe in giving time to reflection, thoughts, and organizing their space.

Introverts, on the other hand, are more reflective and contemplative by nature. Since they are inward-directed, a lot of their time is spent in diligently organizing, arranging, managing, and prioritizing their things. These things give them more clarity of thought and ideas upon reflection. Most people, however fastidious about cleanliness, have concealed spaces that are a complete mess.

These are generally areas that aren't frequently accessed. If these inaccessible areas are kept sparkling clean too, the person is most often suffering from deep-seated anxiety of nervousness disorder. These people are generally control freaks who are obsessed with the idea of controlling things around them to an unhealthy level.

Research also reveals that a disorganized, chaotic, and unclean environment indicates creativity and innovativeness. People living or working in such messy and disorganized conditions tend to generate forward-thinking, resourceful, and path-breaking solutions. Yes, the cliché about a scientist, writer or artist sporting a messier look and unkempt hair may actually be true from a personality-psychological angle.

Colors

What do colors within a person's immediate space reveal about him or her? The first thing that people probably look at when they enter someone's home or office is the color scheme used to do up space. Bright, dazzling, and bold colors instantly draw our attention to space while cool colors create a softer and tranquil atmosphere. An individual's color choice can demonstrate a lot about their personality. For example, if the person has an inherent penchant or bold and vivid colors like red, purple, orange, magenta, and others, they may be more adventurous, experimental, and risk-taking by nature. They aren't shy of expressing their thoughts and are constantly seeking new experiences. It signifies an outgoing, gregarious, unafraid, and bold personality. These people aren't afraid to call a spade a spade.

On the other hand, people opting for cooler and more subtle shades may be reflective, quiet, restrained, and analytical by nature. They are generally deep thinkers, who do not make hasty decisions. Their decisions are made after considering all possible options.

People who are inward-focused will most likely have their homes done up in soft, subtle and solid hues, marked by muted patterns. Extroverts, on the other hand, tend to opt for more old, vibrant, and experimental prints. Since they are more social and gregarious by nature, there is an inherent need to impress people. Extroverts are more outwardly focused, which means their decisions are more determined by what they think will please people around them.

Introverts seldom display this need to impress others and will often downplay themselves and their surroundings in a bid to avoid being noticed. Unlike extroverts, they are uncomfortable at the prospect of being the center of attention.

Prints and Designs

It may sound funny (or intriguing if you are like me). However, the prints or designs used to do up a person's home or office décor or even their attire can be very telling about their personality. For example, bright, bold, large and vibrant prints can signify an uninhibited personality that is more self-assured, opinionated, and seldom overwhelmed by other people's opinions. These people are fiercely original in their thoughts, opinions, and actions. They often have their own opinion on multiple issues and are rarely influenced by the thoughts, opinions, and ideas of other people.

Likewise, quirky prints such as graffiti, pop art, animal motifs, and polka dots can reveal a penchant for fun and creativity. It is an indication of a creative, independent thinking, and original personality. The person isn't afraid to express themselves and is least concerned about fitting in with the crowd. They yearn to stand out rather than fit in. These are your path-breakers, rebels, and trend-setters.

Geometric prints can demonstrate an inclination towards order, symmetry, and organization. People who wear a lot of geometric prints or have their homes/offices done up in predominantly geometric prints may reveal an affinity for balance, orderliness, and analysis. There is a deep-seated need to have everything in order.

In an interesting study conducted by Yale researchers, it was revealed that people who spend hours taking showers or in the bath are generally lonely or emotionally deprived people who seek warmth from the bath to compensate for the emotional warmth in their lives. Makes sense, doesn't it?

Do you a wall filled with motivational quotes and inspiring messages in your home or office? You may want to read this then. Psychologists have researched that people having a wall filled with inspirational quotes and messages are more often than not possess neurotic tendencies. These people utilize their environment or the space around them for soothing their nerves and helping them navigate the storms in their lives. Of course, don't automatically assume that something is not quite normal about a person when you spot a wall filled with motivational posters. The best way to gather more clues is to talk to the person. Observe verbal and non-verbal clues carefully to gain deeper insights into their personality.

Old Stuff

Ever noticed how some people's homes resemble a junkyard because they store all the old and unwanted stuff? There are old uniforms, sports jerseys they've long outgrown, clothes that don't fit them any longer and other memorabilia that has no place in their current lives. These are most likely folks who are unable to discard their past and move on. They are unable to let go of the past and move ahead. There is a need to cling on to the past and a refusal to look into the future. Hoarding objects may mean that they are still emotionally connected with memories attached to these belongings.

For example, if you are still holding on to a dress that you've long outgrown because it was gifted to you by a former lover, you are probably unwilling to come to terms with the fact that the relationship is over. You are still emotionally clinging on to the relationship instead of moving on and looking into the future. There is a tendency to be closely attached to people and memories that these objects represent at a subconscious level.

Chapter 4: Judging by the Cover

"Form is everything. It is the secret of life"
- Oscar Wilde

When you walk into a book store, how do you judge which book to pick up and which to pass? If you are like me, you are guilty of picking up books that have fancy titles, attractive covers and lots of visually arresting features. Accuse me of being shallow, but I also look at the quality of the paper. Yes, judging a book by its cover is something we've all done at some point or the other.

We've all been fed on the belief that judging a book y its cover is not the right way to do it. However, in a time and attention pressed world, where we rarely have the time to read people comprehensively, we seldom have an option but to analyze and speed people to make quick decisions about them. Reading a book by its cover or speed reading people may not be such a bad thing in today's times. People's outer appearances can often help you make solid and reliable conclusions about their personality. The subconscious visual that you form about an individual through their appearance is often accurate.

I know plenty of psychologists who believe that making snap judgments about people based on their appearances is an extremely narrow way of looking at it. However, the way a person treats himself or herself just as he/she treats his/her immediate environment can reveal a lot about their inherent personality. It can help you gain a deeper understanding of their personality to make communication even more meaningful.

The way a person dresses or maintains their outer appearance can reveal a lot about their internal feelings. Their exterior can often be a near accurate indicator of their thoughts, emotions, and feelings. Ever noticed how when you are completely dejected or sad, you don't bother about how your hair or face looks? You don't have the inclination or zest to look good.

Similarly, when you are feeling more positive and upbeat, you will invest extra effort in looking good and feeling wonderful about yourself. People are well-dresses or sport a neatly-groomed appearance to gain respect or validation from others. They may want people to perceive them in a more positive light. It can also be a sign of high self-confidence, power, and authority. People in positions of power and authority may also be wealthy, which gives them the resources to be expensively dressed and groomed. It can be a sign of influence, power, and confidence. These folks are viewed in a more positive or flattering light by other people.

Here are some tips for reading people through their cover or outer appearance to make a near-accurate analysis of their personality or behavioral characteristics.

Good Influencers and Negotiators

Imagine a scenario where a plain-looking person is selling you something you don't really need. He/she is plain looking and not very attractively dressed or groomed. Would you buy from him or her? The person doesn't appear like they are in a commanding or influential position when it comes to negotiations.

Now imagine another scenario where an extremely attractive, well-dressed, and nattily groomed salesperson walks up to you and introduces themselves to you. Again, you don't really need what they are selling but you still listen to everything because the person is cute-looking, friendly, and speaks with oodles of charm. By the end of their sales pitch, you realize that you can, in fact, use the product they are selling.

Attractive and well-groomed people have the power to influence people's decisions, however hollow it may seem. Of course, it isn't simply about wearing good clothes and looking good and ignoring everything else. There is a natural confidence and ease with which these people operate. Other factors such as friendliness, conversational skills, intelligence, and other things matter, too. This should explain why some people invest a bomb in maintaining their wardrobes and appearance.

Introverts and Extroverts

Extroverts thrive on adventure, new experiences, and risks. Their brains process dopamine starkly different than it is processed in a person who is more inward driven or introverted. These thrill-seekers think fast, act faster and are prone to be more impulsive when it comes to decision making. They will move and walk fast, which means they are at a greater risk of injuries.

This can be slightly stretched to conclude that people who have more injury scars or casts have higher chances of being extroverts. Their thrill-seeking disposition and brain make them more prone to accidents and injuries. Yes, these are the people who won't think twice before jumping out of a window to escape an adulterous confrontation.

Similarly, while introverts are more likely to observe your shoes and look at your feet while talking, extroverts will look you directly in the eyes while speaking. Since introverts are more inward driven and reflect upon their options before making a decision, they tend to seize/observe people. There is a tendency to look down at a person's feet because of the awkwardness involved in looking away from a person while speaking rather than looking into their eyes. To avoid this uncomfortable situation of looking everywhere around the eyes, introverts will glance at a person's shoes or feet while thinking.

Since extroverts are more outward driven and focused, they will look people in the eyes while talking. There is a tendency to experience rather than think, which means all their efforts are directed towards experiencing or listening to people instead of thinking about what people are talking about. They'll seldom look in different directions (unless they are lying or there's another clear reason for the mismatch in behavior) and will have their eyes firmly fixated on the person they are speaking to.

Blue eyes and light, blonde hair has almost always been closely linked with introversion. However, there isn't a conclusive study to support this view. More than anything, it is a popularly peddled media notion that is completely supported by the Hollywood and Disney brigade.

There is a definite bias towards light eyes and hair each time a character has to be represented as an introvert. Ariel, Belle, and Hercules are all Disney characters who've been portrayed as introverts with light hair and eyes. Today, you can't go about judging people's personalities through the color of their eyes or hair because people are dying their hair and changing colored contact lenses faster than you can say personality.

Reading People Through Their Clothes

Like we discussed earlier, the manner in which a person dresses reveals a lot about their personality. Neatly dressed and groomed people may have an inherent need to be respected and accepted within their social group. They may have a deep need to fit in or be validated by others. At times, dressing excessively well or paying too much attention to one's appearance can be a sign of narcissism or self-obsession. The person may also be suffering from a deeply-rooted inferiority complex or low self-esteem that they are trying to compensate for by dressing well.

Sometimes, people who pay too much attention to their grooming and appearance may believe that they aren't good enough for anything and may use their looks to cover up for the perceived inadequacies in their life.

One of my friends could never match up to her older sibling when it came to intelligence, social skills, and talent. While the parents lavishly praised her older sister for being an intelligent and talented student, she (the younger sibling) wasn't believed to be striking or extraordinary in anything. Throughout her growing up years, she believed she wasn't good at anything and sought constant validation from people through her looks and clothes. She became obsessed with her appearance and spent huge sums of money on grooming, beauty products, beauty treatments, and makeovers.

Thus, an excessive need to look good and dress well can also be a clue to an inferiority complex marked personality. Know more about a person before you make snap judgments about their outer appearance.

However, appearance along with other nonverbal clues can offer you plenty of insights about an individual's subconscious thoughts, feelings, and preferences.

Chapter 5: Reading People Through Their Photographs

"The camera is an instrument that teaches people how to see without a camera"
             - Dorothea Lange

There are no escaping people's pictures in the age of a constantly buzzing social media feed. Like it or hate it, people are going to pictures of themselves. However, the good news from the perspective of a person analyzer is you can gather plenty of clues for speed reading people even before you meet them simply by learning to read their photographs.

Imagine gaining some clues about a prospective employee before they come down for a face or face interview or learning more about a client before negotiating an important deal with them. How about picking the right date by gather insights about his or her personality through their social media images? Every image of a person holds a fascinating amount of information, meaning, and an indication of his or her emotional state. We only have to be perceptive enough to watch out for these clues. Sometimes, we are so overcome by the aesthetics of the image or the photography that we completely miss the emotions behind the image.

This chapter attempts to offer you some insights about how people's photographs can be used for interpreting their values, personality, and behavioral traits. There are some obvious and some subtle pointers about decoding an individual's personality through their photos. You'll learn to find more meaning and context within the images rather than viewing them as random shots.

Do Not Rush

Since photographs capture moments where time freezes, you need to study the image carefully to avoid any biases or inaccurate readings about something that may have happened in a microsecond. This may be contrary to the fast-speed, short span of attention, limited energy, and the multi-tasking disposition we display. Hit the brain's pause button, do some deep breathing and get yourself into slow motion before you begin analyzing people through their images. You need to approach the art of analyzing people with both curiosity and compassion.

Don't leave out any details Look at the entire image. What is it that holds your attention when you first look at the picture? What are the conspicuous aspects of the image? Slowly move your attention and awareness to the other parts of the images. Look at it from different angles and perspectives.

Pull the image closer to your vision to detect elements that would otherwise go unnoticed. There are plenty of subtle details that your eye may miss if you don't view it closely. Turning the image upside down or sideways allows you to view it from an unusual perspective, which can change your entire viewpoint about the image. You'll end up noticing things you wouldn't have otherwise noticed.

Subjective Reactions

What is it that strikes you the most about an image when you see it for the first time? What emotions, feelings, thoughts, and sensations overcome your mind when you look at the image on an instinctive level? Think of a single descriptive word or phrase as a caption or title for the image that captures your spontaneous reaction to the image.

Do you think the picture represents pride, anger, anxiety, relief, frustration, confinement, exhaustion, success, elation, exhilaration, smoothness, rage, sadness, and other compelling emotions? Your gut-level reaction offers a clue on what you are thinking about the person.

While observing or analyzing people through their photographs, one of the most important considerations is your instant or immediate reaction. However, you'll need to go beyond the first impression. You'll have to apply some amount of free association to analyze the person. Through free association, you are focusing on all elements of the image. Here are some questions you can ask yourself to facilitate greater free association to analyze people through images.

What does the picture remind you of?

What is the predominant emotion expressed by the person in the image?

What memories, incidents, and experiences can you pull out from your own state of awareness on looking at the image?

How would you title the image?

However, when you are analyzing people through their pictures, beware against what psychologists terms projection. Projection is an unconscious process through which our own feelings, emotions, experiences, and memories distort our perception of other people we are analyzing. You may invariably end up projecting your own feelings and experiences to them than trying to identify their personality. This is especially true for more ambiguous images. You don't know if you are rightly empathizing with people reading them correctly or simply recalling your own experiences.

Sometimes, our own subjective reactions get in the way of reading people accurately. However, overcome this tricky situation and identifying when your own experiences and biases are getting in the way of analyzing people will help you be a more effective people analyzer.

Facial Expressions

Human beings are innately expressive when it comes to tuning in to other people's facial expressions. What is your first reaction on looking at the person's face in the photograph? Psychologists have recognized seven basic emotions in a person – surprise, contempt, fear, sadness, anger, disgust and happiness. Keep these seven basic emotions in mind while analyzing people's expressions in images. At times, the expressions are underplayed or subtle, which makes it challenging to pin down the basic emotion.

Look for pictures where the person may not be aware that they are being clicked since that can be a more accurate representation of their subconscious mind.

Relationships

Again, you can tell a lot about the relationship between people by looking at their photographs. If a person is leaning in the direction of another person, there may be attraction or affection between the people. Similarly, if people are leaning in the opposite direction from each other, the relationship may lack warmth. If you notice a person clinging on to their partner's arm in almost every photograph, he or she may most likely be insecure about losing their partner. It may reveal a deep sense of insecurity or fear of losing their partner.

Try to predict the relationship between people through their body language in images. This can also be done in any public place where you have some time at hand to check people's body language, relationship equation, and reactions. What are their feelings, emotions, thoughts, and attitudes towards each other? Is there a pattern in the manner through which people touch, lean towards each other or look at one another? Does their body language reveal a lack of connectedness?

One of my favorite pastimes when it comes to analyzing people is looking at the photographs of celebrity couples and trying to read the nature of their relationship and/or their personality through their body language and expressions. I try to analyze if the image reveals intimacy, affection, and positivity? Or it demonstrates tension, disharmony, and conflict? Akeret, a well-known psychologist, believes that a photograph can also predict a relationships' future.

Some signs of comfort include smiling, holding hands, titling head in the direction of their partner. Hip to hip posture may indicate things are going great between the couple. How is the palmer touch? If it is touching with the full hand, the partners are close and affectionate. On the other hand, fingertips or fist touching can be a sign of being distant and reserved. Crossing legs may mean that they weren't very comfortable or open at the time the picture was taken. If you find a person crossing their arms or legs in almost every photograph, they may be suspicious, doubtful, cynical, and unenthusiastic by nature.

Profile Pictures and Personality Traits

A big body of research suggests that human beings have the tendency to assess one another's personality through a quick glimpse.

This is exactly why first impressions are so lasting. It takes us only three to four seconds to form an impression about a person through their verbal and non-verbal clues. Sometimes, they may not even say anything and we can subconsciously tune in to personality.

A recent research study reveals that you don't even have to meet a person once to form an opinion about him or her. All you need is a quick glance at their Facebook or even Tinder profile picture to gauge their personality. Here are the big five personality traits that are revealed through a person's profile picture.

The big five is pretty much the same to a scientific classification of personalities as Briggs-Myers is for recruitment. This personality approach classifies personalities on the basis of five fundamental traits, namely—introversion-extroversion, agreeableness, open to new experiences, conscientiousness, and neuroticism.

A quick glance at your social media profile picture is sufficient for you to rate people correctly on the five fundamental dimensions. In a research conducted by PsyBlog, it was observed through a scientific analysis of the profile pictures of thousands of social media participant personalities that there were very specific and consistent patterns when it came to each of the five personality attributes.

For example, people scoring high on conscientiousness used images that were natural, filter-free, bright, and vibrant. They were not afraid to express a large number of emotions through their pictures. If fact, they displayed a higher number of emotions through their images than all other personality types.

You'll also find people scoring high on openness taking the most amazing shots. They are creative, innovative, and resourceful. They'll play a lot with applications and filters owing to their creativity. Their pictures will be more artistic, unique, and feature greater contrasts. Generally, people who score high on openness have their face occupy more space than any other feature in the photograph.

Extraversion folks will have perpetually broad smiles plastered on their faces. They will use collages and may surround their profile picture with used vibrant images. On the other hand, simple images with very little color or brightness is a strong indication of neuroticism. These pictures are likely to display a blank expression or in extreme cases may even conceal their face, according to the blog.

Agreeable people may often seem to the nicest people to get along with among all personality types. However turns out, they aren't really great photographers. Agreeable people are known to post unflattering images of themselves! However, even with the poor or unflattering images of themselves, they will be seen smiling or displaying a positive expression. The images will be vibrant, positive, and lively.

Chapter 6: Identifying Deception Through Nonverbal Clues

"The tongue can conceal the truth, but the eyes never!"
— Mikhail Bulgakov

When people used to ask me what is what one superpower I would like to develop, I would always say, the ability to spot liars and cheats. No, I didn't have any super detective or FBI aspirations! All I wanted to do was equip myself to be able to determine when people are lying and when they are telling the truth because this can save us plenty of heartbreaks, relationship troubles, deals gone wrong, and soured social relationships. If there's one superpower that can save you a lot of troubles and conflict, it is the ability to spot lies.

Though we can identify liars on an instinctive level, there are some clear verbal and non-verbal techniques that help you identify deception and lies.

Our unconscious or subconscious mind is capable of detecting liars fairly quickly and accurately. Fortunately, liars offer tons of signals through their words, voice and body language that can be quickly caught by an expert people analyzer. Here are some top tips for making you the ultimate lie detector.

1. Head Movements

People who aren't speaking the truth or trying to deceive others make sudden, unexpected, and erratic head movements when they are confronted with a question. The head will retract slightly and move in a jerkier manner. In some cases, it may tilt a little. This happens in split seconds, just before the person begins to reply to your question.

2. The Direction of Eye Movements

When someone is lying, their eyes will generally move towards their right side. The eyes will go up and then move towards the right. This implies that the person is making up information. Since specific functions are performed by certain parts of our brain, the direction in which a person's eyes move can determine the function performed by their brain.

For example, when a person's eyes move to the upper left, we are most likely trying to recall information that is stored in the memory, which means the person may be telling the truth. However, if a person's eyes move to the upper right, he or she isn't trying to recall or extract information from the memory. They are making up information or lying. When you confront someone with a question, their eye movements will reveal a lot about whether they are lying or speaking the truth. The reverse of this true for left-handed people.

In left-handed people, if the person looks to their upper right while thinking, they are trying to recall information from their memory. However, when they look at the upper left direction when confronted with a question, they are most likely making up facts or misleading you.

So, before you term someone a liar, please ensure you know if the person is left- or right-handed.

But it is not just the direction of a person's eyes. Movements such as raising eyebrows or widening eyes is a non-verbal signal of deceit.

People often look and try to pretend they are stunned when their lies are called out. In a bid to appear surprised and shocked at your insinuation, they may widen their eyes or raise their eyebrows. It may be an act to make others feel guilty about accusing them.

3. The Projection Technique

Liars are brilliant at employing the projection technique. When confronted with a question, they will most likely come up with a counter-question after pausing for a while. This is the typical way liars respond. They will pause for a while to buy time, and contemplate their response on being confronted.

This will be followed by an accusatory question directed towards you such as, "Do you think I am a liar?" or "How can you accuse me of being a liar?" or "Why were you snooping around?" and other similar accusatory questions that are specifically designed to make you feel guilty about confronting them.

4. Nervousness

However smart deceivers think they are, they offer plenty of clues through their verbal and non-verbal communication. Watch out for their leg and feet movements because that is one of the most neglected parts of the body, while we are interacting or communicating with people.

Liars can manipulate other signals such as maintaining eye contact or keeping a relaxed posture since the fact that people who are speaking the truth always look you in the eye is now common and a widely shared knowledge. They know that looking into a person's eyes while speaking can make them come across as more truthful.

However, some signals such as faking their leg or feet movements don't happen too effectively since these aren't very visible neither are they noticeable areas of the body. This makes manipulating leg or feet movements near impossible. Plus, it happens at such a subconscious level that it is near impossible to fake. When people lie or try to mislead others, their legs (or even feet) start twitching slightly. They may be fidgeting with their clothes or pretend to brush something off from their shoulders.

Shrugging or slouching are other obvious signs of a liar.

5. Watch Out for Verbal Signals

While non-verbal signals can reveal a lot about whether a person is lying or telling the truth, his or her words can also be extremely revealing. People who are lying generally speak using a slower and more spaced out way. There are plenty of pauses that they use for buying time.

Their speech will most likely have a more uneven or inconsistent pitch. Liars will be more hesitant in the way they speak. Genuine people answer quickly, while false responses come up only after careful consideration of all options. The person will take more time to think about their responses also slow their speech. It takes time to think of appropriate words when you are lying.

Also, people who lie or mislead others have the tendency to detach themselves from the situation. They will deny any responsibility or detach from the occurrence, which simply means, they'll use lesser sentences in the active voice.

They will seldom use sentences that begin with "I" and will often use passive voice or speak in a manner that something happened to them, rather than they did something. Liars will either offer very little details or a lot of details in a bid to cover the fact that they are lying. There is a tendency they will volunteer with plenty of unnecessary details. They'll attempt to throw your questioning in another direction by offering a lot of details, most of which may be irrelevant, just to demonstrate that they are speaking the truth. They hope people will buy their "innocence" if they give long and elaborate answers.

This makes liars use plenty of fluff words and fillers and very little concrete details. They won't offer solid information. Their sentences will be long and yet not offer anything substantial. People who are lying almost always never offer tiny and verifiable details. They will focus more on emotions or how hurt they are or how someone is feeling. The conversation or interaction will be more fraught with an apparent show of emotions rather than verifiable facts. Always confront a liar by asking them specifics, which only someone who is speaking the truth would know.

Even when you spot a clear contradiction in what they are saying and what you know is the truth, let them continue speaking. Give the confidence that you trust their version of what happened and allow them to give you even more clues about their lies. This can be used for confronting them at a later date. Let them go on and on with stories and created versions that will eventually help nail them. The idea is to catch them in their own spun web!

Liars will almost always detach themselves from an occurrence or event and focus on the other person or people. They will rarely use "I" or "me" while constructing their sentences since they are attempting to detach themselves from their falsehood at a subconscious level. They are not recollecting facts from their minds. Rather, they are fabricating lies, which is why they are trying to distance themselves from their version of events. It happens at a very subtle and subconscious level, and they are obviously not aware of it (until they read this book that is!). There is a very strong need to psychologically distance or detach themselves from the situation

6. Physiological Effects

Lying produces plenty of psychological and physiological effects within the human body (which is what is captured by lie detecting machines) such as immediate blood vessel swelling, rapid heart rate, increased palpitations, sweating, the itchy reaction on the skin, and much more. When blood vessels expand or experience swelling, the skin invariably begins to feel scratchy. This is why liars start feeling uncontrollably itchy when they lie. The itchy nose may not be such a myth after all and may have a deep physiological significance when it comes to spotting liars.

7. The Face Touch

The way in which a person touches their face demonstrates whether he or she is lying or speaking the truth. People who are lying will more often than not cover their mouths using their hands. This is a subconscious gesture to prevent spilling out information that they shouldn't or a way for them to suppress the urge of blurting out the truth. When people cover their mouths with their hands, the thumb will most likely be near the cheeks. Some fingers will be spread over the mouth to psychologically cover it up.

Another sign of deception is when liars are confronted with the truth or a question and instead of answering the question, they break into a fake cough bout. This is nothing more than an attempt to buy time for making up tales.

8. How Are the Hands Positioned?

Keeping their hands at the back can be a sign of trying to conceal something. Liars will seldom reveal their palms or make an open palm gesture. People who are transparent, genuine, and speaking the truth will keep their palms wide open, while those who are being deceitful or lying will turn their palms upside down.

It is a subconscious gesture that they have something to hide. Liars will often place their palms in their pockets to avoid revealing them to the other person, which is a near-accurate indication of them wanting to conceal facts.

9. The Voice Raise

When a person's voice rises slightly or starts becoming shakier owing to muscle contraction, the person may be undergoing some form of stress. Their voice inflection may be higher than normal, and there may be palpable tension within the voice. An expert people reader will not miss these clues.

10. Confidence Variance

Carefully observe the variation in a person's confidence when they are confronted with a question or the truth. They may either freeze or become extremely verbose, thus revealing a lack of confidence or control. If you want to get the person to give away more clues about their lies and deceit, employ a technique used by investigators. Rather than making the communication appear like an interrogation, make it more conversational.

Liars more often than not give themselves away completely by being more illogical, sporadic, and erratic in their responses. If you interact with them in a more conversational manner by letting their guards down, they will invariably give themselves away.

11. Observe Person's Shoulders

Sometimes, a person's shoulders diminish or close in while lying. This is the exact opposite of an expanding posture, which indicates power, authority, and self-confidence. By closing in their shoulders, the person is trying to diminish their posture because, subconsciously and consciously, they are too aware that they have done something shameful, which reduces them in stature.

When they know they have done something wrong, the person's confidence invariably reduces. They are almost ashamed of their act, which leads them to form a more diminutive or reduced posture. Liars often conduct themselves with greater vulnerability. There is always fear and insecurity that their lies will be caught, which leads them into hunching posture. When the elbows draw closer together, the individual takes on a posture that makes them look more diminutive in size, which is a sign of low confidence or vulnerability.

12. Microexpressions

Microexpressions occur in split seconds, which makes them tough to fake. It is near impossible to work on or manipulate one's microexpressions even if people can mislead with their regular facial expressions. These happen so fast that there's no way a person can modify them unless he or she is a practiced manipulator who is aware of body language manipulation techniques. Laypeople, however, will seldom be able to fake microexpressions.

When a person isn't speaking the truth, their mouths will become slightly skewed. The eyes will subtly roll right after the person has spoken a lie. This is a near accurate microexpression of spotting deception. Another not so obvious microexpressions are changes in the color of an individual's cheeks, expanded nostrils, increased sweating, lip biting, and quick eye movements in all directions. These are nothing but signals of brain activity when a liar is processing information that isn't true. There are certain reactions in the brain based on the activity that is happening within it. These processes or reactions are closely connected with movements on the face or physiological facial reactions, which leads to microexpressions.

Chapter 7: Body Language of Attraction

"Listen to the women when she looks at you, not when she talks to you."
— Khalil Gibran

You may be insanely attracted to a person but may not have the courage to ask them out owing to the prospect of facing humiliation and rejection. Imagine how easier things would be if you knew if they are as much into you as you are into them. Think of a situation where you've been set up on a blind date by enthusiastic friends, or you find a date online, and really want to know if they are attracted to you. You may go out on a first date and come back not knowing whether the person really liked you or not!

Wouldn't it be nice if there could be a telepathic way to gauge if a person feels truly attracted to you? How can you figure out if a person is genuinely attracted to you or is being plain nice to you because they don't want to hurt you (yes, we've all been guilty of this.)

Can verbal and non-verbal clues help you establish a potential lover's true feelings, emotions, thoughts, and intentions? Can body language be used for unlocking a person's subconscious mind to tune in to their innermost feelings and thoughts about you? Use these secret attraction clues (that I rarely share with anyone) to help you gain and increase social proof and experience more gratifying and fulfilling relationships.

The Attraction Signals

When an individual is attracted to you, they will transmit plenty of feel-good or positive non-verbal clues for you to tune in to at a subconscious level. To begin with, when a person is deeply attracted to you, their bodies will almost always face you.

Everything from their face, the chest to shoulders and feet will most likely be pointed in your direction. The person will lean closer while speaking or interacting with you in a bid to get closer on a subconscious and emotional level. When they stand at a distance of under four feet away from you, they are keen on entering or personal space or inner circle of friends. They are trying to physically enter your inner zone or personal space to make a place for themselves in it.

If you want to know if a person is keenly into you or interested in you, don't give in to their interest straight away. Rather than facing them, maintain a shoulder to shoulder position. If the person is truly interested in you, he or she will make an effort to win your attraction. Let them know that they have to win your attraction for you to stand facing them or mirror their attraction signals.

Leaning in the direction of a person is almost always a sign of attraction. We subconsciously lean towards people we are attracted to. When a person leans towards you in a group, it is clear that they are interested in you (or what you are speaking). Of course, sometimes a person may be simply keen on listening to what you are saying, in which case, you will have to look at other clues. However, leaning towards a person within a group setting is a subconscious indication that they are drawn towards you.

Another sign of attraction includes seizing a person from up to down, and then down to up.

This is a primitive way, yet still practiced, for checking out the sexual potential of a prospective mate.

Together with other clues, uncrossed arms and legs can be a sign of attraction. Similarly, a broad smile, dilated pupils, and open palms can also reveal attraction. Head tilting is another sign of interest and engagement. It signals a person's desire to communicate to you that they are always around for you. Looking at a person in the eye for long while speaking can also be a huge sign of attraction. If you are attracted to a person or want to win their affection, avoid looking over their heads or even all over the place. It reveals a lack of interest and sensitivity, which will not give them the right signal.

Touch

Touch is a clue that an individual is completely comfortable in your presence.

They may also be keen or getting to know more about you. They may get flirtatious or hit on you by playfully touching you. Some of the most common initial attractions signals are placing their hand over your hand, brushing their shoulder or leg against your shoulder or leg while talking to you and pretending to touch you accidentally.

If you are confused about how to read a person's touches, observe how they touch another person versus how they touch you. If they are generally touchy-feely with everyone around, it is their baseline personality. However, if they make special exceptions in the manner in which they touch you, it is more often than not, a sign of attraction. If the individual touches more than normal or in a different way, he or she may be attracted to you.

If you are attracted to a person, use body language to your advantage by conveying your feelings through non-verbal signals. Don't distance yourself from the person even if you don't want to send out very obvious signs of attraction. On a subconscious level, they may not realize they are attracted to you. Similarly, don't go all out and make the person step back in discomfort. Maintain a balance. Start with a light or playful tap on the shoulder or elbows. It is harmless yet reveals that a person likes you. Then gradually, move to touch their arm, wrist or back while talking. Make the touch more gradual and subtle so they don't wince or retreat with discomfort.

Mirroring

Mirroring happens at a deeply subconscious level and is one of the most reliable signals of a person's attraction. Watch out for people mirroring your actions. There is either a deep-seated need to be accepted or they are truly attracted to you. Sometimes after you've just met or been introduced to a person at a party, you'll notice that he or she starts mirroring everything from your words to your nods to your hand gestures to expressions.

People who don't know much about reading or analyzing people will often miss these clues. However, on a subconscious level, this is a sign that the person is seeking your acceptance or approval. When you are leaning against the bar, you'll notice a person come up to you and lean in the same position as you before striking up a conversation. They are doing nothing but attempting to mirror your actions in a bid to make you feel that they are one among your kind. People will hold their glass exactly in the manner in which you are holding yours or they may take a sip on their drink right after you do to show you that they are like you. The feeling of affiliating with people on a psychological level drives people to mirror their actions.

Chapter 8: Ultimate Nonverbal Clue Cheat Sheet

"To acquire knowledge, one must study; but to acquire wisdom, one must observe."
— Marilyn vos Savant

It is often said that people convey much more through what they leave unsaid than what they actually speak. It couldn't be any truer. It is easy to say what we don't really mean, but because that is controlled by our conscious mind. However, it isn't easy to hide nonverbal clues about what we are thinking or feeling because that is more of an automated process, which is governed by our subconscious mind.

Therefore, tuning in to these clues helps us connect with a person's subconscious, which is more challenging for him/her to control and manipulate, unlike words.

When we communicate with people, we are constantly giving and receiving wordless signals. All our nonverbal clues, including our facial expressions, gestures, the tone and pitch of our voice, the speed with which we are talking, gestures, eye contact, proximity to the other person, and much more convey powerful messages even if we aren't aware of it. Often, these messages do not come to a standstill when we stop talking. Even in our silence, they end up communicating a lot.

People have much less control over the nonverbal messages they convey than what they actually speak. Nonverbal communication is more of an instinctive, emotional, and reflex reaction that is more trustworthy than mere words, which can be consciously manipulated at will.

If there is a clear mismatch between what a person says and how he says it, nonverbal communication is generally granted more weight because it is hard to stage-manage.

According to research, people retain about 10 percent of information given orally and about 20 percent of information given visually. However, 80 percent of the information given in combination (oral and visual is retained), which means people who communicate both orally and visually have a higher chance of putting their point across more persuasively and effectively.

Body language and other nonverbal clues are just as important (or in fact more) when it comes to reading and analyzing people. People are capable of retaining what they see more effectively than what they hear, which means if you are looking to analyze a person, pay close attention to their body language and other nonverbal clues.

When nonverbal cues match a person's words, it's a sign of trust, confidence, clarity, and a comfortable rapport. On the other hand, when the non-verbal and verbal cues don't sync, it creates an atmosphere of mistrust, frustration, confusion, and tension.

Why, even lack of clear nonverbal messages is a telltale indication than the person is carefully manipulating his body language in order to hide his real feelings and emotions, which speaks a lot on itself.

Here are some proven tips and powerful guidelines for acing the nonverbal clues games.

1. Look for a Clusters of Clues

One of the biggest mistakes people make while analyzing body language is looking for standalone signs, without viewing a cluster of clues. It works wonderfully for slick poker player flicks, but not in real life. One often has to view a group of signs or actions to come to a reasonable conclusion about a person's feelings or behavior. For instance, a person may be making eye-contact, and you've been trained to believe that making eye contact is a sign of confidence. This means you ignore all other signs such as sweating, constantly touching one's face, etc. that reveal nervousness.

Always look for a cluster of clues rather than a single non-verbal clue. It is easier to manipulate a single clue than a bunch of everything else pointing to a clear thought or behavior pattern.

Spotting one cue shouldn't make you jump to an instant conclusion. For instance, a person may be leaning in the opposite direction from you not because they aren't interested but simply because they are uncomfortable. If you are depending heavily on non-verbal clues, ensure that you spot at least three to four signs pointing to a clear thought process or behavior.

Try and take cues from different non-verbal communication sources. For instance, you may want to collectively analyze someone's tone, facial expressions, posture, hand gestures, etc. to be sure your analysis is accurate. Working in clusters increases your chances of reading an individual's behavior accurately.

2. Establish a Baseline

It is important to have a clear reference or baseline for someone's behavior to analyze them well in general. There will be instances, of course, where you will be meeting and analyzing people for the first time. However, by getting to know someone better personally gives and makes your insights even more powerful. It gives a more well-rounded and wholesome approach to the analysis process.

Let's consider an example. One of your close friends is a very fast-thinking, swift-acting, and fidgety person. He is high on energy and forever bouncing ideas off people. Someone who doesn't know this friend too well, or doesn't have a baseline for judging him will inaccurately interpret his fidgeting as a sign of nervousness.

If you were to spot him on the street as a complete stranger, you'd believe he was nervous as hell. However, since you now have a clear baseline to understand he's hyperactive and excited about everything, you won't wrongly interpret his fidgety ways as nervousness.

Pay close attention to people's behavior all the time to understand their baseline. How do they behave and react in various settings? How is their speech and communication pattern in general? Are they in the habit of looking people in the eye? Does their voice undergo a transformation when they're particularly nervous? How do they react when they are deeply interested in something? How do they communicate when they are preoccupied or disinterested in something? These are critical points when making an effort to read people. It eliminates all the potential fallacies you can make while analyzing people.

When you spot inconsistencies in their regular baseline behavior, it will be easier to tell something is amiss. It will help you keep an eye out for nonverbal communication patterns that are not in sync with their regular behavior.

3. Body Language Cues

Though this is a huge subject by itself that has consumed realms of paper and ink, let's get straight to the most crucial points. An individual's body language can convey a lot about how they think or feel. For instance, leaning forward or towards your direction when you are talking communicates that the person is listening to you keenly, and is interested in what you're speaking.

Similarly, limbs placed at the sides are an indication of being relaxed and in a positive frame of mind. Maintaining eye continuous eye contact is, in general, a sign of confidence, honesty, and positivity.

Similarly crossing limbs while communicating with a person depicts the person is not open to or interested in what you are talking about.

They are more shrouded in secrecy and not transparent by nature. Tapping fingers on the table of feet on the ground can be read as a sign of high nervousness. Similarly, when a person looks away while talking, he or she is almost always resorting to some sort of deception or is simply not interested in talking to you.

Crossed arms or legs are like barriers that indicate that the person isn't really in agreement with your ideas or what you are saying. Even if their expressions are pleasant or they are smiling, these physical barrier signs can be revealing. They are psychologically blocked from what you're saying. What makes this or any nonverbal near accurate is that the process doesn't happen intentionally; it is more involuntary.

4. Touchy Tales

Observing how people touch you can give you plenty of insights about their behavior, and how they feel about you in general. Though touch is a tricky one since most people have their own ideas about touches based on their personal bubble. However, like most body language cues, it can give you a good idea about what the other person is thinking or feeling.

A weak handshake, for instance, could indicate uncertainty, hostility, or nervousness. Similarly, the proximity of a person to you while you are speaking is a good indication of their interest in what you are saying or their feelings for you. People often distance themselves from others while talking, when they don't wish to be intimate, affectionate, or vulnerable.

Research by the Income Center for Trade Shows reveals that if you shake hands with an individual, the chances of them remembering you double. People view you as being more friendly, warm, and welcoming when you shake hands with them.

While as a general guideline this is true, also take into consideration a person's baseline behavior. He or she may not be very comfortable being in close physical proximity to people, regardless of the circumstances. Therefore, in such instances, a person maintaining a distance from you doesn't speak as much about you as it does about them.

Famous Hollywood talent scout/agent Irving Paul Lazar is famously quoted as saying that, "I have no contract with my clients. Just a handshake is enough." It speaks volumes about things you can judge about a person from their handshake.

5. Tone Tell Anyone

The tone of an individual's voice can convey heaps about how they are feeling. Listen closely for any inconsistencies in the pitch or tone of a person's voice. Are they coming across as predominantly excited or angry? Are they trying to hide something?

The volume of one's voice is also a reasonably dependable indicator of how a person is feeling. If a person is taking louder or softer than usual, something may be amiss. Closely observe if a person is using more fillers than concrete words and sentences. It may be a huge indicator that they are hiding something, nervous, or trying to simply buy time to fabricate stories.

Sometimes, people's tone conveys very strong emotions that they are trying to hide or not expressing straightaway. For instance, a person may say the sweetest thing to you but the tone can be more sarcastic, caustic, or grudging. These may be the passive-aggressive folks, who feel the need to address people or situations in a less aggressive manner.

Since about 80 percent of our entire message is communicated nonverbally, note other's words to read or analyze them. The meanings of some words can transform entirely when announced differently, thus making voice tone and inflection an important criterion for analyzing a person's behavior.

For instance, something as simple as the way you end a sentence can communicate a lot about how you are feeling. When you end the sentence an elevated note, you're turning a statement to a question, or approaching the statement with an element of suspicion or doubt. This makes a person appear less assured and authoritative than intended.

6. The Cultural Context

Though some body language cues like eye contact and smile are universal, many nonverbal clues have a clear cultural context or baseline. For example, Italian culture involves overtly expressive gestures such as plenty of waving, loud talking, excited voices, and shouting.

In Italian culture, excitement is more conspicuously expressed than, say in the UK. The nonverbal communication pattern is much more upbeat and loud, which can make it hard for the Italians to interpret the behavior of someone coming from a predominantly British or American culture, where the excitement is more subtly expressed. Therefore, viewing things in a cultural backdrop is important, especially if you're involved in doing business or forging political relationships with other cultures.

Even seemingly similar gestures can have an entirely different meaning in another culture. For example, while the thumbs-up sign (yes, the same gesture through which we seek approval and validation on social media) is a symbol of validation in English-speaking nations, it is considered inappropriate in some regions of the Middle East and Greece. Similarly, while making an "o" sign with your forefinger and thumb is signifies OK in English-speaking nations, it is considered a clear threat in Arabic nations.

Personal space is almost sacred in the Western corporate culture, so respecting associates and clients when they put up some barrier (like a bag or purse) is important. The amount of executives and managers who lose out on business deals for not interpreting these clues isn't even funny.

In addition to the cultural context, consider the overall context of the situation or circumstances under which the behavior occurs. Some settings (like a job interview) require a more formal behavior, so sitting in a particular posture or gesticulating in a particular manner should not be misinterpreted. It can simply be attributed to the demands of the situation.

For instance, your body language at a pub when you are out with co-workers on Friday evenings varies considerably from your body language when you're with them at work. Non-verbal signals will vary according to the situation, so try to ensure that when you're analyzing people, you're also taking the situation into consideration. This will prevent you from wrongly reading a person who is spending a relaxed Friday night with co-workers as laidback, non-serious, and disinterested.

7. Identifying Deception

It is both easy and tough to spot deception in a person. Easy if you look for the right cues and know how to probe. It is tough because signs of deception and nervousness often overlap. However, it's important to read people and know exactly when they aren't speaking the truth.

Typical cues of lying include:

- maintaining minimal eye contact
- constricted pupils
- fingers on the mouth while speaking
- faster than normal eye movements
- the person usually tries to physically turn away from the person they are addressing
- increased breathing rate,
- face and neck region complexion changes
- increased perspiration

- change in the manner of speaking such as stammering, pitch elevation, and clearing throat

When you notice any or all of these signs, don't instantly jump to the conclusion that the person is lying. A majority of these cues can also be signs of nervousness or fear (can be true in situations such as a job interview). If you want to ascertain if a person is lying, simply probe further and ask more questions to give yourself more time to determine the truth based on both verbal and non-verbal clues.

Reading nonverbal cues will vary from person to person. It comes only when you practice people watching and reading body language on the train, airport, and television (by turning off the sound). Closely notice people's actions and reactions.

When you observe them, try to decipher what they're thinking or trying to say. When there is a group of people, try to decode who the influencer or leader of the group is, and get a feel of what they are discussing among themselves.

Even when you don't get an opportunity to gauge whether you are right or wrong in your analysis, you'll still develop a sharp, trained, observational eye, which will come handy while communicating with others.

While watching out for the above-mentioned clues related to deception, it is also important to keep the person's baseline personality in perspective, along with cultural context and their behavior in other settings. Avoid making sweeping conclusions.

Some people are naturally awkward and nervous by nature. They tend to exhibit pretty much of the behavior mentioned above at regular intervals. Therefore, is important to determine how the person normally behaves. If their mannerisms, gestures, and eye movements are always a bit awkward, that's their personality.

Closely observe their body language and eye movements when you know for sure or have already established that they are speaking the truth. Compare or contrast this with their mannerisms when you suspect that they are not telling the truth. When you observe continuous change while making certain statements, you'll quickly gauge whether they are recalling facts/information or simply cooking up stories.

8. Nonverbal Cues on a Date

Assume it is your first date with someone. Can you imagine how incredibly helpful body language can be in helping you gain insights about the person's behavior/personality, which can, in turn, determine if he/she is a good match for you? Obviously, it's not easy reading people on first dates. Everyone's trying to put their best foot forward. You're also trying to be as charismatic as possible while also expressing your interest in listening to what the person is saying. Where is the scope for analysis here?

Pretty much like everything else in life, with a little practice and keen eye, you'll learn to spot the right signals effortlessly, without investing too much time.

It isn't rocket science or anything overly complicated. Just tune in to simple things like how guarded they are with their bodies. Initially, everyone will appear guarded. They will most likely cross their legs or arms and keep a fair physical distance from you. The palms will generally be held facing them. This is reasonable on the first date.

However, as an observer, you'll have to determine if it slowly transforms into a more open, warm, and welcoming during the course of the date as the comfort level between you and the other person increases considerably. By observing their body language, you'll quickly know if they are genuinely interested in what you are saying, and that if they are naturally connecting with you by demonstrating a more open body language.

We have a tendency to mimic or mirror other people's behavior. So if you want the other person to look and feel more relaxed and less tensed, take on a more relaxed posture yourself. They will most likely mirror your actions and match your behavior.

Leave your arms uncrossed, give an honest smile, avoid physically distancing yourself from the date, and reveal your palms. These cues convey that you are warming up to the other person, which will also make him or her comfortable. Of course, the level of comfort will keep fluctuating during the course of the date, and it will be nerve-wracking to maintain a standard demeanor. If you observe that a particular topic is stimulating a particularly negative body language, stop in your tracks and change the subject quickly.

9. Eye Contact

Renowned among lovers all over the planet, Shakespeare wasn't off the mark when he famously quoted that "the eyes are windows of the soul." Indeed, one of the most powerful nonverbal communication tools us eye-contact between two people. Maintaining consistent eye contact between people reveals trust, openness, genuineness, and sincerity.

Little eye contact during negotiation can prevent you from building a good rapport with the other person. If conveys to the other party that you're not being straightforward, are acting evasive, and worse—you aren't honest.

Similarly, analyzing the other person's body language can give you insights into their personality or behavior. Are they avoiding your gaze? Are they acting more shifty and fidgety? They may not be the best people to do business with, in that case.

Again, you need to spot a cluster of clues and not isolated nonverbal clues. Also, look for any inconsistencies in the person's verbal and non-verbal clues. For example, a person may be fidgeting because he is nervous or new at this. He may just be hired to negotiate on behalf of an organization and this may be his first project. When you look for other clues, you'll realize that the person is simply nervous and not necessarily dishonest. It is also natural to shift gaze when a person is involved in deep thinking or information processing.

Too much eye contact can also signify aggression, power, and a more threatening approach. The other person may be trying to intimidate you by maintaining continuous eye contact.

10. Proxemics

Proxemics refers to the subject of personal space maintained between two people when they interact or communicate face to face. How many times have you felt uncomfortable when someone tried to stand too close to you while talking? The person is obviously trying to gain acceptance or validation from you or trying to make it into your inner circle.

Get others to respect your personal space and respect theirs, too. If a person tries to come too physically close to you during negotiations, he may be trying to intimidate you or subconsciously coerce you into accepting his proposal. If you want to test a person's comfort level before making any move, simply stand or sit at a minimum of four feet away from them, and observe them closely to guess their comfort level.

If they look more open and welcoming, you are being invited into their personal space. If their body language is more rigid and closed, give them more time before jumping into their personal space.

11. Mirroring

Mirroring is mimicking or imitating the other person's nonverbal communication patterns subtly. When interacting with people or meeting them for the first time, check if the individual is subconsciously mirroring or mimicking your actions or behavior.

For instance, if you are seated across a table from another person, and suddenly rest your elbow or palm of the table, do they follow suit? Observe closely for about 10-15 seconds to check if they are subconsciously mimicking your actions.

Similarly, when you lift a glass to take a sip of water or drink, does this person follow your actions? If yes, it's good news. If someone is constantly mirroring your body language, they are keen on establishing a warm rapport with you or seeking approval from you. Try adjusting your actions or gestures to observe if the other person follows suit. You'll know soon enough if they are keen on establishing a rapport with you.

Chapter 9: Communication to Read People

"You don't have to tell me what your limits are when the decisions you make, your actions and body language says it all."
— Marlan Rico Lee

Verbal communication is everything that is conveyed through written and spoken language. On the face of it, it may seem easier to decipher than nonverbal communication; however, people are also experts at faking what they say, so its interpretation becomes slightly tricky and more meaningful only when combined with nonverbal communication.

Sometimes relying only on non-verbal clues can be tricky, and you will need verbal clues to complement the nonverbal clues for gaining a better understanding of someone's exact motives, behavior, or personality. Imagine if you saw a person imitating a bird's flapping movement without knowing the setting or context. How would you interpret it? The person could be playing some game, he could also be demonstrating the movement of birds to someone, he could be drying himself, or he may be living in an altered state of mind where he thinks he's a bird.

There are innumerable interpretations of a person's behavior and movements, which is why you cannot solely rely on nonverbal clues or body language for a comprehensive interpretation of a person's behavior or personality. You also need to probe further and watch out for verbal clues that reveal more about their motives, behavior, and personality.

For instance, a person may not be feeling too positive or upbeat, but may simply say they're not too bad. In this scenario, it is important to watch out for both verbal and nonverbal clues. Their words and the manner in which those words are uttered may point to the fact that they are in fact not too good.

In the above example, if the person says "not too bad," it can be interpreted as they aren't too good either. Of course, the person's regular verbiage and culture will determine how they usually speak, but their selection of words can reveal a lot about how they are feeling.

Let us consider another example. You open a nice new specialty restaurant in the heart of the city and have a steady stream of diners pouring in to try out the new dishes. Since the venture is still in its initial stages, you're eager to obtain feedback from your new customers to work upon areas that need improvement.

You head to a family who has just finished eating their food for their feedback. The woman promptly says, "The soup was good." How would you interpret this? It can mean the soup was exceptionally good. However, there are higher chances that it means that nothing else was noteworthy except the soup.

When you learn to watch out for verbal cues, you're training yourself to read between the lines. People will often not spell out everything. They'll expect you to read their thoughts and feelings based on subtle verbal clues. For instance, don't we all hold a small grudge against people who say, "You're looking good today. " And we're doing the internal eye roll emoji thinking, "Don't I look good every day? Why just today?" Some positive souls will interpret it as this means I am looking exceptionally good today.

There are plenty of hidden clues in what people say; you just have to listen and watch keenly to comprehend the right meaning.

Talking Too Much

Talking too much can be both—a sign of authority, or a sign of trying to evade the real issue. It becomes all the more conspicuous when the conversation is peppered with a lot of fillers (ah, umm, hmm), silences, and repetitions.

People who are trying to hide something or deflecting from the real issue aren't generally very concise in their verbal communication pattern. They try to buy time by hammering the same point repetitively using different words and phrases.

Confident people in positions of authority or leadership seldom talk fast or in an incomprehensible, rambling manner. They spread out their words, their tone is more even, and speak in a clear, audible, and coherent manner.

Similarly, people who are more self-assured, honest, and open will convey things in a more concise, crisp, and unambiguous manner. They may not always use the right words (dependent on language abilities); however, they'll communicate in a more coherent and synchronized manner. Their sentences are less peppered with gap fillers and ambiguous words and phrases that are more open to interpretation.

Verbal Modeling

It is human nature to be drawn to people who are similar to us. We naturally take to people who share the same interests as us, come from a similar cultural background, possess the same attitude as us, and even speak like us.

Therefore, people who are constantly trying to match your words and talking speed may be eagerly looking to be accepted by you or please you. Doesn't this happen during job interviews?

Sometimes the interviewer is talking too fast, and the interviewee, in his attempt to please the interviewer, picks up the same speed or ends up choosing the same words and phrases subconsciously. This is referred to as mirroring in psychological lingo. You are simply mirroring the other person's words, actions, and attitude to impress them or demonstrate that you're just one of them.

Acknowledgment

A person who is keenly listening to you, cares about you, or is interested in listening to you will almost always throw in verbal acknowledgments in the form of "yes", "yeah", "I understand how you feel", "wow", "sure", "really" etc.

These verbal interjections and acknowledgments communicate that the person has heard you out and understood what you're trying to convey. People who are disinterested or don't care about what you're trying to convey will be less likely to come up with acknowledgment words and phrases during the process of the conversation.

Beware if the acknowledgments are too frequent or over the top (if this isn't the person's usual baseline personality); it can be more contrived or fake.

Paraverbal Clues

Since we've already discussed this in the previous chapters, how they are can be abundant scope for misinterpretation while deciphering verbal clues. Paraverbal clues (similar to nonverbal clues) help in adding more authenticity to our analysis.

Paraverbal clues comprise everything from tone to pause between phrases to the speed of one's speech to the volume in which a person speaks.

Fast-paced speeches can reveal a more deceptive, disorganized and uncertain demeanor, which is highlighted by ambiguous words and phrases. An evenly tempered speed can be an indication of self-assuredness, assertiveness, and balance. This person knows exactly what he wants, and is confident and comfortable expressing himself.

Similarly, a high voice volume can indicate authority or leadership. The person is trying to convey that he is in charge of the situation or trying to persuade people to accept his point of view or demanding attention.

There are several other verbal cues you need to watch out for while reading people. For instance, some expressions or sounds are used to complement words to make the message even more effective. Sometimes, the message is too intense to be conveyed only with the help of words, which means you need to watch out for sounds like screaming, laughing, sighing, and moaning to interpret the message accurately.

Word Clues

Notice how people are almost always dropping clues through their words. For instance, imagine a person has just stated that he's won another award. When you pay close attention to the choice of words, you'll realize that the person is trying to convey that he's won an award or several awards prior to this. He wants to ensure that people know he has done well previously too; thus, boosting his image.

This person may be the kind who is constantly seeking validation, appreciation, and adulation from others to boost his self-esteem. He is likelier to be exploited using flattery and ego-boosting praises.

Incongruence in Verbal and Non Verbal Cues

People can say anything they want and they often lie through their teeth because they get away with deception. However, when you spot incongruence in a person's words and body language or expressions, you know something is amiss. For instance, someone is mentioning that they are really fond of someone, and while saying it, they are almost involuntarily shaking their heads.

Notice how people sometimes say something makes them extremely happy, yet while saying it, their expression is painfully somber. This can be revealing. However, don't jump to any conclusion until you are able to gather more information.

Practice your skills by watching chat shows or talks shows by turning the volume down. Try to guess what these people are saying simply by observing their expressions, gestures, and posture. When you're done writing what you think they are saying, watch again. This time turn up the volume and check if their words were congruent to their expressions or body language.

Pay Attention to the Emphasis

You may not be a trained FBI agent but there are still lots of sneaky tricks and clever strategies that can be used to read people accurately. One of the most important verbal communication cues is the word a person emphasizes while speaking. This reveals a lot about what is important to him along with his choice of words.

For example, if your supervisor says, "I've decided to go ahead with this idea," and emphasizes on the word "decided", there's little anyone can do to change his mind. He's conveying he has already made up his mind and that there's no further scope for communication. Words reflect our thoughts and feelings.

The words we use are loaded with meaning, which consciously or subconsciously ends up revealing plenty of underlying emotions. Similarly, the words a person uses can a lot communicate a lot about his personality. It is an indication of a personality that's not impulsive, more thoughtful, and analytical. Look out for words people use (especially action words) while talking to you. It will tell you more than people think they are giving away.

If someone constantly emphasizes the word "hard" in saying, "I worked hard to accomplish this," or it is "hard work", they are most likely goal-oriented folks who love a good challenge and do not like to be given things on a platter. It also suggests that the person is capable of delaying gratification or holding off pleasure until they achieve the results they are after.

If a job application is constantly using the term "hardwork" (yes I know they all do and they lie too, in which case you have to look for a combination of clues to spot inconsistency in their verbal and nonverbal clues), he may be a more goal-oriented and diligent employee, who doesn't shy away from taking up challenges or big responsibilities. He may possess the required determination to finish the given assigned tasks and can be dependable.

However, you have to be careful in situations like interviews where people are aware that their personality, body language, confidence, etc. are being assessed in a more controlled and closed environment. This gives them the ability to manipulate the actions and body language to create the intended impression. However, if you have a trained eye and some practice, you'll quickly detect any inconsistencies.

Chapter 10: Effective Tips and Tricks for Reading People

"The highest activity a human being can attain is learning for understanding, because to understand is to be free"
— Baruch Spinoza

Now that you've gained some expertise in analyzing people's behavior, let's sweeten the deal and give you even more amazing tips and tricks to read people like books.

Here are 12 amazing strategies that will give you insights into what people are thinking and feeling to help you understand them better and develop even stronger interpersonal relationships.

1. Even seemingly innocuous questions such as, "How are you today?" may be an attempt to establish your baseline thus, setting the stage for further probing and inquires. This technique is typically used by salesmen and business associates. If you're trying to establish someone's baseline, gently probe them about how their day was, or how they are doing today. It opens the gates for further discussion, probing, and negotiation.
Ask more open-ended questions if you want to set an initial baseline for interpreting people.
2. Former FBI agent Navarro offered many effective tips on reading people in Psychology Today. One of his tips

included avoiding vague questions after establishing a baseline. A rambling individual is tough to interpret. Therefore, ask straightforward questions that have a direct answer, which makes it easier for the questioner to detect deception. Don't look or appear too intrusive. Simply throw a question and observe, minus interruption.

3. Clues that convey discomfort, stress, and distress include a furrowing brow, clenching jaws, compression of lips, and tightening of facial muscles. Similarly, if someone is shutting their eyes for longer than a regular blink or clearing their throat, there's a high chance they're stalling. Leaning away from you or rubbing hands against their thighs or head is also a sign of high stress.

4. Children are brilliant subjects to practice on when it comes to detecting liars. If you're looking for signs to spot a liar, simply observe what children do when they lie. Annie Duke, a renowned professional poker player, and cognitive psychology doctoral student suggested that kids are an excellent source to pick up cues about deception. Adults pick up deception skills to bolster social interactions and personal relationships, which kids haven't mastered at that stage. Therefore, they are pathetic at lying. Every sign is clearly visible because they aren't yet adept in the art of lying. Therefore, observing clear signs of deception in them gives you the ability to spot the same signs in adults.

This, of course, comes with its own fine print. Some people will be better at lying than others. Those who have mastered the art of deception will obviously be well-versed in hiding signs of untruth.

5. When someone nods excessively or in an exaggerated manner, it means he is simply conveying his anxiety about your opinion of him. The person is also likely to think that you aren't confident about their abilities.

6. Our brains are hard-wired by default to interpret power or authority with the volume of space occupied by someone. For instance, an erect posture with straightened shoulders conveys authority. It communicates that you are occupying the optimum available space.

   On the other hand, slouching is occupying less space and presenting yourself in a more collapsing form, thus, demonstrating reduced power. People who maintain a good posture automatically command respect on a subconscious level.

7. Genuine smiles are easy to tell apart from contrived or exaggerated smiles. When a person is genuinely delighted to see you or by the conversation they're having with you, their smile reaches the eye. It also slightly crinkles one's skin to form crow feet. Smile is the single largest arsenal people use to hide their true feelings and thoughts. If you want to tell whether a person is smiling genuinely, watch out for crinkles near the eye corners or crow's feet on the skin. The smile is most likely a deception in the absence of these signs.

Did you know that a genuine smile is called Duchenne smile? It is believed that a smile can never be faked no matter how hard a person tries. Have you ever wondered why you or someone ends up looking so awkward in pictures? It may appear on the fact that we're smiling, but we're actually only pretending to smile. Since a genuine smile elevates your cheeks a bit, there are bound to be some crows feet, which bundles up just below the eyes. Body language experts say this is tough to fake.

You actually need to experience a happy or joyful emotion to be able to create that expression. When you're not comfortable from within or not experiencing genuinely happy emotions, the expressions just do not fall into place.

8. Look out for micro expressions. If you observe people closely, you'll notice

that their real thoughts or feelings, and not what they're trying to deceptively convey, will be flashed on their face in the form of micro expressions.

Sometimes, while trying to come across as consoling, they'll quickly let off a smirk that can last 1/15th of a second. This is because their thoughts and expressions are syncing involuntarily for a moment.

Next time you're traveling by aircraft, notice how flight attendants smile with the help of their mouth but their eyes are blank, and the eyebrows are in a positioned in a scowl when you ask for more drink.

The truth almost always slips out in the form of these tiny expressions or micro-expressions. While it isn't difficult to fake body language, look out for the not so subliminal cues, which are a clear giveaway. It's pretty much like shooting stars; you've got to see it fast before it disappears.

9. Avoid making assumptions. One of the best tips you can receive while analyzing people is not to make prior assumptions or have any sort of biases or prejudices. Sometimes, we go to analyze people with a clear prejudice and think we've already found what we've been seeking. For example, if you assume (based on prejudices etc) that a person is angry, then all their actions and words will seem like there's a deeply hidden anger within them. You will find only what you are looking for. For instance, if we go to a person's workplace assuming that he is totally disinterested in the job or dislikes it, we'll assume his concentration or lack of cheery approach as absolute

disinterest in the job. He may be strictly trying to focus on his job as opposed to hating it. Not everyone grins and laughs when they are enjoying their work. Sometimes, they are just involved in performing it more diligently.

Another important point is to avoid judging other people's personalities based on your own. For instance, in the above scenario, if you truly love your job, you'd have a more positive, grinning, and happy expression as opposed to a more somber look. However, not everyone shares your unique traits, behavior, attitude, beliefs, and values.

10. Identify behavior patterns. Take for instance you're flying in an aircraft and a particular cabin crew member looks really pissed off while talking to a

passenger seated near you. Now, you can quickly jump to the conclusion that he or she has an inherently arrogant, impatient, and hostile personality. However, he or she may have just fought with his or her partner before boarding the aircraft and may still be carrying the anger within him or her. You really can't tell if it's the former or latter until you observe a clear or repetitive pattern.

Does she look particularly annoyed when passengers ask for something? Well, then you've spotted a pattern. If not, you're just being plain unfair in judging him or her based on a single isolated pattern that originated due to another external situation (argument with her partner.) Looking for patterns helps you analyze people more objectively and accurately.

11. Compare behavior. When you've noticed that someone is behaving particularly out of sync within a group of people or in a specific setting, observe whether they display the same behavior in other groups, too. Also, if someone is acting slightly off the normal course with a person, try and gauge if they repeat the same actions with others, too.

Continue to observe the person's actions in multiple settings to gain a comprehensive insight into his personality or behavior. Does the individual's expression or gestures change? Does his posture undergo a transformation? What about the voice and intonation? These clues help you know if the behavior you observed initially is a norm with them or simply an exception.

12. Notice people's walk. The way a person walks can reveal a lot about him. People who are constantly shuffling along demonstrate a clear lack of coherence of flow in things they take up.

    Similarly, people walking with their heads bowed reveals a lack of self-confidence or self-esteem. If you do observe one of your employees walking with their head down, you may want to help build the person's spirit.

    Appreciate him more in public and give him tasks that demonstrate your faith in him. Approach him by asking him open-ended questions during meetings to get him to talk more and bounce ideas off people.

13. Power play with voice. Much as people like to believe, the most powerful or commanding person is not the one at

the helm of the table. It is the person with a confident, firm and strong voice. Confidence denotes power.

At any conference table or business lunch, the most powerful and influential/persuasive individual is the one who has a confident and commanding voice, and huge smile (smiling is a sign of effortless confidence almost like the person is so good, he doesn't have to try too hard). However, do not confuse a loud voice with a confident/strong voice. Merely speaking loudly won't earn you respect if you sound shaky and confused. When you're pitching an idea/product to a group of decision-makers or people in general, watch out for people with the strongest and firmest voice. These are the people the leader may generally rely on for making decisions or these are the group influencers. When you learn to observe and identify the strong voices, your chances of a positive outcome increase drastically.

People in power often keep their voice low, relaxed, and maximum pitch. They don't speak in a tone that elevates in the end as if they are asking a question or sounding uncertain/doubtful about something or looking for approval.

They will spell their opinion in a more statement like manner by employing a more authoritative tone that elevates in the middle of a sentence, only to drop down in the end.

14. Stand opposite a mirror to observe your own body language. Give yourself various scenarios (party, informal outing with friends, a business presentation) and start talking like you would in these settings.

Being aware and conscious of your own body language in varied settings will help you identify patterns on other's body language too. Not just the mirror, the next time you find yourself at a negation table or first date, try to be more aware of your body language and the impression you are trying to convey. This will help you decipher the other person's thoughts and emotions more effectively through their body language.

Observe your own body language without being self-conscious or judgmental. Look how your eyes light up when you are talking about someone you care for deeply. Notice how your eyebrows raise when you are speaking to someone you don't really like or trust. This will help you gain a better understanding of other people's thoughts and feelings.

Notice everything from your eye movements to gestures to posture. This will help you understand exactly what you need to watch out for while analyzing other people.

By tuning into your own underlying feelings and emotions, you will be able to judge other people's body language, words, and actions more accurately.

15. When people try to manage their body language by misleading others, they concentrate on their postures, facial expressions, gestures, and postures. Since their legs movements are more unrehearsed, this is where you're most likely to find deception. When in stress and duress, they will display signs of nervousness, fear, and anxiety with their legs.

If you watch closely, their feet will fidget, shift, and wrap around each other make increased movements. The feet will involuntarily stretch, kick and curl their feet to eliminate tension. Research has revealed that people readers will enjoy higher success analyzing a person's emotional state just by observing his or her body. Even though you may not be aware of it until now, you've been intuitively responding to leg and foot gestures all the while.

Chapter 11: Personality and Birth Order

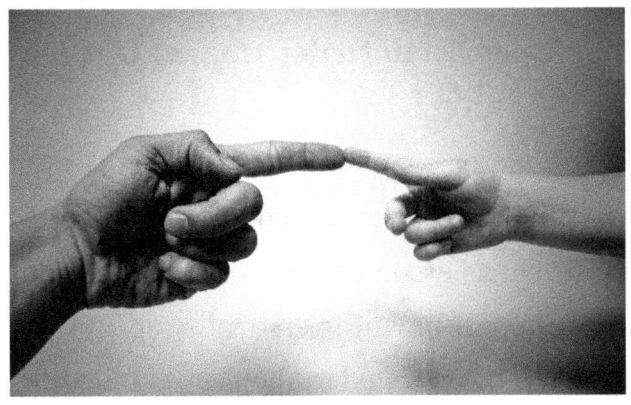

"A brother is a friend given by Nature"
— Jean Baptiste Legouve

Nope, the effect of birth order on personality type is not just pop psychology, BuzzFeed quiz-style talk. It is in fact based on consistent research and scientific principles. Chuck aside the entertainment and stereotypes, and you have a near accurate technique for determining someone's personality. There are plenty of psychological principles behind the amusing stereotypes that determine people's personalities depending on their birth order.

Why Does Birth Order Impact Our Personality?

According to some psychologists, birth order is as crucial as genetics in determining an individual's personality. It boils down to the nature versus nurture personality debate. Research has pointed to the fact that birth order can indeed influence our personality owing to the fact that the way parents relate to every child of theirs (based on his or her order of birth) is different. Children from the same household never assume the same role.

There is always a clear demarcation of roles and equations between the parents and children vary based on their birth order. For instance, if you are the oldest among siblings and assume the role of a caretaking sibling, no one else will fill that role. The others will then pick other roles, says an achiever or provider.

Parents are almost always directed by a different approach at the birth and subsequent upbringing of each child. The firstborn instills a sense of pride and paranoia in parents. If you are a parent, you'll understand how frightened you were at each potential injury of your firstborn. Similarly, the middle born is often bossed over or dominated by the firstborn sibling, who is already sufficiently acquainted with the ways of the world. The older sibling is viewed as wiser, responsible, and competent.

Compared to the firstborn, the other children are less likely to be micro-managed by the parents, thus changing the equation between them slightly. Parents are more exhausted and worn out by the time the later siblings arrive.

They most likely realize that their fears are unfounded and that the baby doesn't really need to be micromanaged. Thus, parents turn slightly more flexible when it comes to disciplining and attending to later children. Therefore, middle and younger siblings learn to attract attention.

It isn't a biological process where just because you jumped out of your mother's tummy first, you are destined to be a leader. Rather, it is about how the parents treated the child depending on this birth order that leads to the child developing a specific personality.

Since the firstborn is more of an experiment for the parents, there is a greater tendency to be overly obsessed with minute details, thus leading the child to be a perfectionist. On the other hand, the youngest born child is born when the parents have already figured things out.

The youngest child is also competing for attention with older siblings, which makes him more of a people please and less obsessed with the idea of perfection.

The First Born

The firstborn child in a household is often believed to be ambitious, dominating, and responsible. They are known to be natural leaders and often lead by example. These are the folks people often look up to for guidance and solutions. They operate with a deep sense of responsibility and are goal-driven.

Since firstborn children enjoy undivided attention, at least for some time from their parents, they are naturally used to being in the front or limelight. They feel like there's no competition and that they are born to lead. It can be seen as a byproduct of the attention showered on them in the absence of other siblings.

The firstborn child may connect more effectively with other firstborns than his or her siblings owing to the birth order. Parents often rely on their firstborns to assist with taking care of their younger siblings, which makes them responsible and reliable.

They are more often than not well-behaved, meticulous, caring, and conscientious. This comes from the idea that others rely on them. From childhood, they've been conditioned to believe that others are dependent on them for support and guidance.

It isn't surprising then that they turn out to be high achievers who constantly seek validation and appreciation from others. They also tend to have a dominating personality and are perfectionists by nature. The older siblings assume the role of a mini parent while also being insecure at the prospect of losing the parents' undivided attention.

The Middle Born

The general notion about middle born children is that they have a high sense of fairness and peace.

Middle children are generally understanding, adjusting, co-operative, yet competitive. They are likely to have a close set of friends, who give them the attention they've not got from the family. Middle children often receive the least attention and affection from the parents, which makes them turn outside the house for forging more meaningful relationships.

They are generally late bloomers and find their calling after much deliberation and experimentation. However, middle born people are often at the helm of powerful and authoritative careers that let them use their slick negotiation skills. This helps compensate for all the attention they probably didn't get as children.

The personality traits of a middle child are diagrammatically opposite to the characteristics of the first and young child. However, they are unique, juxtaposed between siblings and this role makes them expert negotiators. They quickly learn to navigate their way through tricky and awkward situations. This equips them for entrepreneurship and other positions of authority.

Youngest Child

By the time the youngest child is born, the parents are fairly assured of their expertise as caregivers. They are no longer paranoid or hesitation about their skills as parents. This makes them more flexible and lenient towards the youngest child. There isn't a tendency to monitor every move of the child, which makes more independent. Younger siblings generally enjoy more freedom and thus become independent thinkers and decision-makers. The youngest and oldest children have few traits in common because they've both been brought up with a high sense of self-entitlement.

They've both been made to feel special based on their oldest and youngest positions in the household. Younger siblings have always learned to deal with their parents' divided attention. They are fairly adept at handling competition and aren't bogged by feelings of insecurity and jealousy. They operate with a sense of security and often know their place.

Since the parents are more flexible with them, youngest born people often tend to follow their hearts calling. You will find them in more creatively stimulating professions such as stand-up comedians, actors, painters, writers, and dancers.

The youngest born tends to take more risks, have an untamed spirit, and are often exceedingly charming. If someone tells you they are the youngest sibling in the family, they almost always know how to wriggle out any situation by using their charm. Don't forget to overlook the context though when you're analyzing people.

Sweeping judgments don't work very well when it comes to analyzing people. There may be several things to consider such as situation, setting, context, and culture. In your over-enthusiasm to read people, you may end up making incorrect observations by overlooking context.

The Lone Rangers

Yes, I know what you are wondering. What if you happen to be the only child and don't fit into any order of birth? Lone rangers or the "only child" is often more mature and confident. They tend to think beyond their years owing to the fact the lone rangers are almost always surrounded only by adults in the household. In the absence of siblings, much of their interaction is only with grown-ups of the household.

Having spent a lot of alone time, they become more confident, independent, solution-oriented, creative, and resourceful. Lone rangers have a lot in common with firstborn children. They also share the self-entitlement and feeling of specialness that is associated with the youngest siblings.

Is It Always True?

It may not always be true because parents are known to set extremely high expectations for the firstborn. When first born children do not meet their parent's expectations, they can become highly rebellious. There is a rejection of his or her role.

It is true that most middle born children are excellent peacekeepers and negotiators because they neither have the rights of the oldest sibling nor the special privileges of the youngest sibling. Caught in the middle, they learn to negotiate their way through life and become exceptionally good peacemakers.

They are more emotionally connected to their friends, owing to the fact that they don't receive the desired attention from the family. They tend to become social butterflies who spend more time outside the house.

It is a known fact that parents aren't as stringent or careful about their youngest child since they are fairly experienced in raising children. They have already seen their older children grow with the required trial and error, and are hence more at peace. A majority of the time, parents are more financially independent by the time their youngest child is born. Thus, the overall feeling of contentment, security, and leniency towards them is high.

Sometimes, the youngest children don't fancy being the baby of their household. There is an increased need to be taken more seriously. This drives them to be more serious about their responsibilities.

Always pay close attention to how people refer to their birth order while speaking about it. Do they appear more positive or negative about their position? This reveals a lot about whether their birth order has been a bane or boon while influencing their personality. Similarly, observe people's body language while they are speaking about their birth order.

Factors Impacting This Structure

Birth order is not a precise science for determining an individual's personality. It is a good practice to try and know more about an individual's siblings if you are trying to read their personality based on birth order. In addition to birth order, there are several other determinants of who a person turns out to be.

The Natural Elements

Genetics is the single most influential determinant of an individual's personality. About 50 percent of who we are is determined by our genetic make-up. A majority of our personality is influenced by natural, in-born factors.

Gender

Other than birth order, gender also influences who we become or the roles we assume within our household. For instance, if the firstborn is a son, and the second born is a daughter, they will each have their own gender-based identity.

The daughter will not be bogged down by the pressure of living up to the boy's accomplishments and responsibilities. If the second child was a son, he would've probably experienced the pressure of living up to the older man's achievements. However, since it is a girl, the pressures are not as marked since she will have an identity of her own based on her personality.

Communicating With People Based on Their Birth Order

First Born

Firstborns on account of their undivided attention status, at least for some years, tend to be dominating, leading and controlling by nature. There are in fact two categories of firstborns. The first is the rule-abiding, responsible, and the compliant firstborn type who strives to be an example for their siblings.

The second category is aggressive and dominating leaders who know how to get things done owing to their perfectionist ways. Be a good team player, follow the rules, and demonstrate a caring approach towards the former category. Similarly, seek the expertise, and stick to perfect ways of the second type. The leaders enjoy being in control and issuing instructions, so you need to be a good follower while dealing with them. They derive a great sense of importance when people ask for expertise or guidance.

Middle Borns

Middle borns are often known to be rebellious by nature since they do not enjoy the special privileges of the first and last born. They often do not get the attention enjoyed by the firstborn or the special pampering received by the second born.

Showering them with special attention or offering genuine compliments is a great way to get into their good books. They tend to be either outgoing or lonely. Try to win the confidence of the lonely middleborns without pushing them to open up.

Give them their time and space, and you'll do well. Do not rush them into anything. Similarly, if you're negotiating with them, you better be excellent at the game because middleborns can be exceptionally gifted negotiators.

Handle the rebellious with gentle firmness. Be assertive yet polite while communicating them. They are good at compromising in any situation, which is why they also quickly take to peacemakers and solution providers.

Avoid confrontation and deal with them in a more sensitive, and accommodating manner. Learn to be more compromising and adjusting while dealing with them.

They may have issues with assertiveness, confidence, and self-esteem. Keep this mind while interacting with them. Boost their self-esteem while interacting with them, and you'll win brownie points with them.

Last Borns

Last borns on account of being "the baby of the family" generally become less self-reliant and independent compared to their siblings. They can often be unrelenting and stubborn. The best way to deal with them is to shower them with attention and affection. They are happy to take suggestions and advice because they aren't very independent thinkers. Don't try to negotiate with them as when they make up their mind, they are almost always sure.

Chapter 12: Body Language Reading Tips To Slay Your Next Negotiation

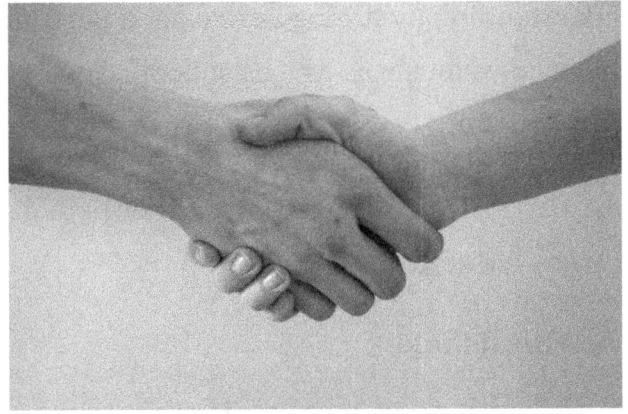

"Information is a negotiator's greatest weapon"
                          - Victor Kiam

Like any social scenario, you are interacting across verbal and nonverbal channels. It literally results in two simultaneous conversations at one time. According to research, people send more than eight hundred distinct nonverbal clues over half an hour of negotiation.

If you focus only what the person is saying, you are losing out on a whole chunk of the message. Construct a brilliant bargain by understanding by tuning in to what a person is saying consciously as well as subconsciously.

Here are a few tried and tested tips to ace your next negotiation by reading the other person or party accurately.

The Handshake

There have been volumes written about the perfect handshake. A firm handshake on meeting the person or being introduced to him or her is an indication of confidence, self-assuredness, determination, and courage. A business associate or potential client who shakes your firmly is subconsciously trying to convey to you that they are up for the negotiation game and are more or less firm in their decisions. Clutching a person's hand too tightly can be read as a sign of aggression, superiority, power, or intimidation.

On the other hand, a limp handshake symbolizes lack of confidence, low self-esteem, lack of clarity or low determination.

Mirroring

If the other person mirrors your actions, gestures, tone, or words, it is a positive sign they are keen to impress you or buying what you say. The prospect or business associate is most likely engaged. They will lean forward or mimic your movements. When people aren't taking to what you are saying or are switching off, they'll lean back.

Their arms and legs will be crossed. Find a way to draw the person into the conversation and find out why they are closed to what you are saying. Don't go any further when you find a person crossing his arms and legs. Try to get them to uncross their arms and legs or they'll subconsciously not absorb what you are speaking.

Head Nodding

Frequent head nodding is a sign that the other party is eager to gain your acceptance or validation. They are ready to do what you are saying to impress you. A person who maintains eye contact while nodding continuously implies the negotiation is going in the right direction. It is a sign of diffusing hostility or tension and creates a sense of being on the same plane with the other party.

Nervous Gestures

People tend to reveal their stress or nervousness through their hands. Fidgeting, twiddling, or clasping hands is a huge sign of nervousness. If you are trying to make an important or powerful point, keep your hands below the chest. Pull or entwine your fingers to make the point in a more confident and forceful manner.

Firm Feet Planting

Again, the feet are the most non-obvious part of the body while reading a person's body language, which is why we tend to overlook a lot of revealing feet or leg movements. If people's feet are firmly or resolutely placed on the ground, he or she is firm about their point. They are resolute and not likely to change their stance. It is also a sign of high confidence, security, and self-assuredness.

Maintaining Personal Space

As discussed earlier, the field of proxemics involves focusing on the distance between two people while communicating. A person standing too close to you may be attempting to coerce or intimidate you into accepting their point. It can also be a sign of attention and interest.

The feeling of hostility is less marked when the person maintains a minimum distance of four feet from you. It indicates they respect your personal space or are not trying to physically intimidate you. They are giving you an option to make your decision after weighing all facts and figures.

Look at the Hands

Hands are the most expressive parts of our body, which means, it adds plenty to the meaning of the message. As a thumb rule, if the person is rubbing their face, they are generally nervous or anxious. Similarly, when a person is keeping his or her hands on the mouth, they may be lying or concealing some important information. If the person keeps his or her hands away from their face, they are confident and truthful.

Hands left loosely in a relaxed position at the side of the body is a positive sign that the person is comfortable about what is being said. They are listening to you in a relaxed and positive manner.

Leaning

If a person has an open posture and leans in your direction, he or she is keenly listening to or interested in what you are saying. They are also interested in knowing your opinion or take on the points they have presented.

Read Them While Reading the Document

When you want to judge a person's thoughts or feelings about the deal, pay close attention to their body language while explaining the contents of the document or clauses. When the person tells you to go through a document, ask them to highlight its contents.

Tune in to their body language while they are going through the contents. It can be extremely revealing. You will know whether they are misleading you, trying to be manipulative, or genuinely interested in offering you the best.

Even experienced negotiators tend to deflect their attention on paperwork rather than focusing on people. They miss vital body language clues by not being alert and focused, and pouring over documents.

Chapter 13: Recognizing Personality Type

"Tell me to what you pay attention and I will tell you who you are."
- José Ortega y Gasset

People analyzing is an intriguing and exciting process. It helps you unlock clues to a person's mental process that no one except he or she has access to. You will go into mental spots that were previously unreachable.

What's the number one tip when it comes to reading or analyzing people? I'd say, do not look for standalone or isolated clues. Watch out of a cluster of clues while considering the context.

People who are feeling cold may hug themselves or cross their legs and arms. If you're jumping to conclusions at stand-alone clues, you'll conclude they are not open to what you are saying or mistrustful. However, they are simply cold. This leads to a serious discrepancy between facts and your analysis.

You need to understand the person's fundamental or basic nature to establish a clear baseline for reading his or her behavior. Ask yourself questions such as, "Is this the individual's regular behavior?"

Do they generally display this behavior in a similar situation? What is driving them to act in a specific manner? This helps make your analysis more foolproof.

To make accurate assessments of people while reading them, look at a cluster of different verbal and nonverbal clues rather than heavily relying on a single indicator. Also, don't use people's situational behavior to determine their overall personality.

For example, a person may come across as increasingly aggressive or dominant while talking to someone who is bullying their (the first person's) child. This is because their parental instincts are at play. The person may not possess an aggressive or dominating personality. Thus, many a time, people's behavior is contextual.

Cluster of Clues

Look out for a group or cluster of clues if you want to read a person more accurately. For instance, if you want to establish whether a person is lying, look at his eye movements, his feet, his speech pattern, the inflection in the voice, the words or verbal expressions used, facial expressions, hand gestures, and more.

Observing a bunch of clues gives you a more reliable reading than catching single clues.

When multiple clues point in the same direction, you will be more confident of an accurate conclusion.

Similarly, if you think a person is nervous, just because they are twiddling their thumbs, check for others signs of nervousness such as perspiration, hesitant speech, using gap fillers, and more. For all you know, the person may simply be restless or hyper-energetic by nature or plain bored. Avoid making the fallacy of jumping to a conclusion when it comes to reading body language clues.

If a person is stepping back when you confront them with a question, they could be lying. If their voice quivers while replying and they step back. They are more likely than not being deceptive.

However, reply in a quivering voice, step back behind and offer plenty of extra details, you can almost be certain they are lying.

See what we did there? We are just looking for more clues to make an assessment more accurate. For all you know, the person may be stepping back or shifting their feet because their shoes are uncomfortable. Based on this single movement, you may conclude that the person is lying.

It is pretty much the same when you are assessing someone's overall personality. Don't make assumptions based on isolated situations. Observe them in multiple circumstances before coming to a conclusion about their personality type.

The Four Temperaments Theory

The four personality theory is a proto psychological concept that talks about four primary personality types. It divides people based on sanguine choleric, melancholic, and phlegmatic. People with a sanguine personality are enthusiastic, socially-driven, and active.

Similarly, people with a choleric personality are impulsive, short-tempered, easily irritable, and quick to anger. Melancholic people are analytical, logical, and calm. Similarly, phlegmatic folks are serene and relaxed.

Most personality theories are a combination of two or more of these four basic temperaments. The extent to which each temperament is present in an individual determines their personality. Every person is a mixture of more or less these four fundamental personality traits.

Though the theory that bodily fluids influence four dominant human personality types was later rejected due to lack of evidence, a majority of personality classifications use similar categories for classifying personality types.

The DISC Concept

The DISC personality classification method is based on the idea that each person is distinctively different from other people in the way in which he or she thinks and perceives the world.

Everyone isn't similar to us, which is why we're left wondering what a person was thinking when they decided to do or saying something. Isn't it common to say things like, "Oh but why did she or he do that?" or "What was he or she thinking when he or she did that?"

What we are doing is evaluating a person's actions based on our personality, without realizing that their perspectives and thoughts are wired differently from ours. Yes, no one is like you. Notice how you can say something to five different people and elicit five different reactions from.

You said the same thing, but they all perceived it differently based on their personality or temperament. Thus you've got five different reactions to the same question. Think of it this way. There's a different chip fitted in the brain of every individual, which helps them perceive and process information in a manner that is different from others.

Take into consideration that different isn't in terms of good or bad. It is just different. Everyone is wired differently, which means someone different from you isn't necessarily bad. He or she just doesn't see things the way you do or vice-versa. A lack of understanding of this leads to plenty of heartburn and missed communications goals. It can lead to disappointment and unmet expectations.

There is a fairly simple and effective model for understanding complicated human behavior. It is referred to as The DISC Model of Human Behavior. It'll help you understand the minds or personalities of people to develop more rewarding people skills, which leads to more fulfilling interpersonal and social relationships.

Think how rewarding it would be to minimize conflict in any relationship and focus on productivity? How about being able to understand or relate to people more effectively?

The DISC model of human behavior is based on a couple of fundamental observations about people and their behavior. The first observation is that some people are more outgoing than others. There is an inner motor that drives people to "quickly go for the kill," while others have a more gradual pace. People are essentially outgoing or reserved.

The second basic difference is people are either people-centric or task/work-centric. According to the DISC personality model, we are guided by an external focus that determines our behavior. While some people are task-oriented or action-focused, others are more clued in to the people around them. Again, there's nothing like good or bad and right or wrong.

The four primary personality characteristics identified from the above discussion is: outgoing, reserved, task-oriented, and people-oriented. Now, each person possesses these qualities in varying proportions. Using a combination of these four fundamental personalities, there are four quadrants created to reveal four basic personality types, which have descriptive expressions beginning with D, I, S and C (hence the name DISC).

- -The first quadrant is people who are outgoing and task-oriented
- -The second quadrant is people who are outgoing and people-oriented
- -The third quadrant is people who are reserved and people-oriented
- -The fourth quadrant is people who are reserved and task-oriented

Let us attempt to understand each personality type.

People in the first quadrant are the dominant "D" folks who are outgoing and action/task-oriented by nature. They are always emphasizing on getting things done, achieving goals, accomplishing challenging tasks, and quickly getting to the point. They invariably make things happen. The key to forming a great relationship with "D" type people is results and deep respect for their authority or knowledge.

The "I" type person is outgoing and people-oriented by nature. He or she is heavily focused on enjoying people's company, socializing and having a blast. This personality time is focused on other people's opinions of them. They are deeply affected by what people think or say about them. Give them admiration, support, and recognition, and you'll enjoy a rewarding relationship with them.

The supportive "S" personality type is a combination of reserved, people-oriented folks. These people enjoy helping others and working in teams. They also find it gratifying to form solid interpersonal relationships. The best way to win them is by demonstrating a caring, friendly attitude, and offering sincere compliments.

The cautious "C" personality people are reserved and task-oriented. They are focused on consistency, reliability, quality, and accuracy. They are detailed and focus on facts. The key to developing a rewarding relationship with these folks is earning their trust and operating with a sense of integrity.

Connecting With Every Personality Type

Since each personality type has unique characteristics and areas of focus, it is important to understand how to connect with each type to establish more fulfilling relationships. Here are some well-researched tips.

Give "D" people the confidence that you value the end result as much as them. Be focused on the result while doing any task, and come up with a bunch of proactive solutions. They also appreciate when people come up with suggestions on how a task can be implemented more efficiently.

Respect their views. Don't challenge their opinion or views in public. Instead, offer solutions and suggestions gently in a manner that shows that it is beneficial for the overall task ahead. The "I" person is outgoing and people-focused. They are forever nervous about what others are thinking about them, which gives you a great opportunity to put their doubts at rest. Offer "I" people sincere compliments and positive/constructive criticism. Compliment their appearance, clothes, and external persona.

They are won over by admiration, appreciation, and recognition. Ensure you don't take them for granted and appreciate what they do. "I" folks are happiest when their efforts are recognized. Appreciate who they truly are, and play them abundant compliments and you'll dwell. Type "I" responds well to praise.

To connect with the "S" type personality, you need to have a friendly, caring, and approachable stance. They appreciate warmth, selflessness, and friendliness in a person. Since they themselves are naturally helpful and dependable, they expect others to be the same. Be there for them during tough times, and you'll win several brownie points with the type "S" folks.

To connect with "C" type people, work on winning their trust. They place a high premium of trust, loyalty, and integrity. It takes some time to be in their good books because they are very picky about the people in their inner circle. Bear in mind that winning them is all about being honest and ethical.

Conclusion

Thank you for purchasing this book.

I genuinely hope it has given you a treasure trove of insights into analyzing people's personality through tried and tested strategies, proven subconscious techniques and several practical, actionable tips. These tips can be applied in setting from business to personal relationships to social settings.

Whether you want to figure out the personality of a potential business partner during a business association or the suitability of a prospective recruit for the given job or the compatibility quotient of a potential date, this book is a handy resource for helping you analyze others effectively. If there's one skill that translates into success in the modern world, it is the ability to analyze people.

This allows you to customize your message according to the personality of the other individual to achieve effective communication.

The next step is to use the book and implement it in your daily life in small, slow ways to start with. Start by noticing people at the airport or doctor's when you have more free time.

Finally, if you enjoyed reading the book, please take the time to share your views by posting a review of Amazon. It'd be highly appreciated!

DARK PSYCHOLOGY FOR BEGINNERS

What are the Secrets of Mind Manipulation and Control?

Introduction

It is generally known that knowledge is power. Having said that, possessing human psychology knowledge should be equated to having superpowers. Psychology is the scientific study of the mind of human and how it functions. Psychology covers a wide range of areas including crime to religion, finance, advertising, love, hate, selling and marketing. If you are able to understand the principles of psychology, you have a key to human influence. This is something that is possessed by few people.

To gain psychological knowledge is usually not an easy task as many may think. Just like many of the hidden treasures of man, psychological knowledge is engraved deeply in journals and books. This is of course away from the public's reach. To access this information and make it useful, you may need to go through many journals and books in order to get useful content and separate it from the one that is not useful.

The process of separating has been accomplished. You have access to the finest information which has psychology's most powerful philosophies. All you just need to do is to show your interest in learning, reflecting and practically applying the knowledge you get from this book.

Throughout this book, you will get an insight of the hidden mystery of the world that is understood by only a few people. This is what is referred to as dark psychology. The most powerful influencers use the principles outlined in this book in their journey to being the people they were.

You will know how the principles of the dark of dark psychology are applied. This is of course after getting to know the principles.

Thank you for choosing this book. Enjoy reading!!

Chapter 1: What is the Dark Psychology Story?

Knowing about something that can be used against you gives you agency in those moments when wielding said knowledge can make or break your life. Much like history, your life is probably full of moments where having some insight into dark psychology could have dramatically changed the complexion of your life. There are several good reasons for one to learn about dark psychology. Dark psychology could best be described as a study of the human condition in which it becomes normative for people to pray upon others out of criminal and or deviant desires. Often these desires lack specific purpose and are based primarily on basic instinctual desires. Each human has the potential and capacity to victimize other humans, as well as other living creatures, but most of us keep these desires suppressed in order to function successfully in society. Those of us who do not sublimate these dark tendencies are typically representative of the "dark triad": psychopathy, sociopathy, and Machiavellianism, or other mental disorders/psychological disturbances. In this way, dark psychology focuses primarily on the underpinnings (i.e., the thoughts, processing systems, feelings, and behaviors) that are found below the more predatory aspects of our nature, the same ones that go most vigorously against the grain of modern thought concerning human behavior. In this field, we tend to assume that these more abusive, criminal, and deviant behaviors are purposive most of the time, though there are instances in which they seem to have no teleological underpinnings.

Most people assume that they understand the darker aspects of human nature. They imagine they would be able to see manipulators if they met them and know exactly what to do to keep themselves from being taken advantage of. Most people are wrong.

Evil will not wear a mask that makes it easy to identify. In fact, it will do quite the opposite. It will blend in and gain the target's trust before turning on them and victimizing them. The victim will often realize what's going on when it is already too late for them to do anything about it.

The devil himself is known for taking the ideal form or even appearing as an angel of light.

Users of dark psychology are no different. They are master shapeshifters that will take whatever form is necessary to snare their prey. Disguise and deception come naturally to them. So what does one do then?

The best place to start is by educating yourself on their methods. One does not have to use any of them, but they do have to learn enough so they can at least identify the threat when it is present. That is the first step to solving any problem.

The first thing most people don't realize is those dark personality traits are a part of all of us. As such, we all use them to some degree in our daily lives. People around us may even use them on us in ways that are not harmful to us, not realizing what they are doing. Sometimes they may even use them for our own good. Think of mothers telling their kids false facts to get them to eat their vegetables, or trying to trick a drug addicted loved one to go to a place where they'll find their loved ones waiting to ambush them with an intervention.

Well, this chapter will give you some of the examples that you are most likely to meet throughout your life and highlight many of the tricks they might use on you. It leaves out a lot of the more benign examples of the tricks of dark psychology and tells you of the times when there may be high stakes and you cannot afford to be manipulated or blindsided. These can be moments where someone tries to get you to spend more money than you had intended to, or act in a way that may set you down a path that could be disastrous for you.

Principle

Wrongdoing, as Socrates asserts, is doing that harms others. Not only does this harm others, but Socrates also thought that it harms our own souls, as many modern people would agree. Dark psychologists allow that some of us do wrong onto others for no greater purposes. Their ends never justify their means because there are simply no ends to be found. This capability (and perhaps even proclivity) for harm within cause or purposiveness can be found within all of us. The field of dark psychology assumes justifiably that these irrational desires to harm within us are incredibly complex and hard to understand.

Whether wrongdoing is purposive or even intentional, and whether it is done out of want of money, retaliation, or power, the most destructive force behind wrongdoing is aggression. Aggression is likely the single biggest adversary of prosocial relations, and it should not be confused with assertiveness. Aggression is any verbal and or physical behavior that is meant to harm or destroy. This aim is what differentiates it from other classes of behaviors that bring harm or destruction with no aims.

Biologically, there are certain genetic markers that are more indicative of aggression than others. Neurologically, it is the amygdala that controls most aggressive behavioral patterns. For this reason, people with enlarged and deformed amygdala typically commit violent acts at higher rates. As far as hormones are concerned, it is usually those people (primarily young men) with higher levels of testosterone and lower levels of serotonin who tend to be the most violent. The most aggressive people within societies are typically ones who have been put through something of a loop: their testosterone levels rise and cause them to become aggressive, which in turn begets higher levels of testosterone and even more aggression. In this way, some of the most dangerous people the world has to offer are created. Drugs and foods that increase serotonin and decrease testosterone levels are typically the best options for decreasing overall levels of aggression.

The most common cause of aggression is a failure or being stopped short of a goal. Studies indicate that those who have been made miserable by such unfortunate events usually make others around them more miserable as well. In these unpleasant instances, we naturally become frustrated, which begets our being angered, and once we are angered, we can easily become aggressive if given a cue. Some of the most common stimuli that can cue aggressive behaviors are personal insults (perhaps the most common), cigarette smoke, foul odors, and hot temperatures. Ostracism is another common cause of aggression, causing some of the same neurological phenomena as physical pain does.

Chapter 2: The dark core of personality/Dark Factor of Personality

We seem to concentrate too much on the easier side the of human psychology. Whether those followers of the "positive psychology" movement or not, we often tend to have difficulty seeing the value in the more rank underbelly of human psychology, the dark side. This happens to our detriment though, as it is the more bothersome aspects of our nature that tend to enlighten us more than the personas that people put on. Here we will delve into the darker traits of human psychology, the ones that all contain one overarching trait more destructive than any others: callousness or a lack of empathy for others. Those who have these traits are very diverse, but they all share the potential to harm others due to their inability to empathize.

The first of these traits, and perhaps the most common is narcissism. We all display this negative trait at one point or another, so it is usually best to reserve judgment when others come across as narcissistic upon first glance. Narcissists often disregard the thoughts and feelings of others and take advantage of people in order to get what they want. Witnessing other people getting attention and admiration frustrates them, as they believe that they are entitled to these things above others. This trait, like any other, exists on a spectrum within people, with the most pretentious of us at the top and the ones with least self-efficacy at the bottom.

Although all of us experience narcissistic traits in varying degrees, in around 1% of the population these traits can take on a more severe, pathological form in which the person gains an unrealistic perception of his or her own abilities and is in constant need of attention and admiration. This anthologized form of narcissism is called narcissistic personality disorder.

Narcissistic supply is a sort of admiration, sustenance, or interpersonal support drawn by a narcissist out of his or her environment. This supply can easily become essential to the maintenance of the narcissist's self-esteem if it is never kept from him or her. For this reason, narcissists tend to seek out those who will admire them irrationally and there is very little chance that will stop a narcissist once he or she has found some sort of relationship in which there are unjustified resources allocated interpersonally. This need for the admiration or attention of codependents is considered pathological because it does not take into account the feeling, thoughts, and or needs of the other people involved. The narcissist only considers his or her supply and is never focused on what is actually going on with those other people involved.

Narcissistic injury is something seen as a danger to the so called narcissist's self-esteem. Other terms interchangeable with this one are a narcissistic blow, narcissistic scar, and narcissistic wound. What all of these have in common, however, is what they are met with narcissistic rage. Narcissistic rage is known as a common reaction to any form of narcissistic injury. Now this rage (like any other sort of rage) exists within a continuum, ranging from mild remoteness to harsher expressions of annoyance and frustration, and finally to intense emotional outbursts, sometimes including violent attacks.

Narcissistic rage can manifest itself in many other ways as well. These include depressive, paranoid delusion, and catatonic episodes. It is also widely held that most narcissists have two major types of rage. Mainly the first of type is the rage constantly directed at one or more other people, while the second type is constantly directed at the self. Narcissistic rage is not necessarily troublesome in its severity, as its severity exists on a similar spectrum as does "normal" rage, but becomes more problematic when considering that it is inherently pathological.

The narcissistic defense is any process whereby the idealized self portrait of the narcissist is preserved, while any of its actual limitations are denied. In other words, this type of defense is found when the narcissist is trying to preserve his or her own self-image more so than trying to ascertain the truth about the self. These defenses tend to be very rigid, as the narcissist anchors as much as possible to the most self-flattering narratives imaginable. Most narcissists actually do experience feelings of guilt or shame (both conscious and unconscious) quite often, and one of the most common methods by which they alleviate these negative feelings is by putting up such defenses. Pathological narcissism has to find psychological shortcuts in order to survive throughout greater self-realization, and narcissistic defense is likely the most common of these shortcuts.

The original definition of narcissistic abuse referred more to the abuse committed by narcissistic parents on their children. Typically, this type of abuse consists of the children of narcissists having to give up parts of their own feelings and wants in order to protect their parents' self-esteems. Children who grow up being subjected to this type of abuse often have codependency issues later on in life. Having no knowledge of what constitutes a normal relationship, they tend to be unable to recognize who it is who they will be better off with and who to avoid. It is common that they will formulate further relationships with more narcissists who have similar pathologies to those of their parents.

In more recent years this term has been more widely applied to abuse within relationships among adults. Adult narcissists are about as likely to abuse other adults as they are to abuse children. These abusive relationships typically do not last as long due to the fact that adult victims usually have much more mobility to get out of the relationships than do child victims.

The next dark trait is Machiavellianism. This term can be applied to both the political philosophy of Niccolò Machiavelli and a manipulative personality trait. Here only the later usage will apply. This trait is most commonly characterized by a deceitful personality style, a pathological focus on personal gain and self-interest, an overall deficiency of empathy, and a blatant disregard for morality.

One of the most troubling aspects of Machiavellians is their overall lack of emotion. This often leads them to be influenced very little by "conventional" modes of morality and to subsequently manipulate and deceive others without remorse in order to meet their own personal needs. This trait is measured in units called machs by psychologists. People with higher levels of machs are shown to agree more with statements such as "never tell others your reasoning unless it benefits you to do so", and less with statements such as "people are generally good", "there is never an excuse to lie to others", or "the most successful among us lead moral lives". Typically, males score higher levels of machs than do females.

Machiavellians are typically rather cold and selfish people who see others mostly as instruments they can use to serve their own interests. The motives that they have in mind at any given point in time, whether they be sexual, social, professional, etc., are often pursued in duplicitous manners, with little to no thought of the wellbeing of the other parties involved in mind. Those with higher levels of machs tend to be motivated more by power, money, and competition than anything else, while those with lower levels of machs tend to focus more on things such as family commitment, self-love, and community building. People with higher levels of machs want to win at any cost, no matter how steep. With these views in mind, we could reasonably argue that people who are more Machiavellian than others are also more bent toward avarice. These people are typically much less motivated by altruistic sentiments and any forms of philanthropy, and instead, spend most of their time in aimless competition and malevolent industry. For these reasons, Machiavellians are usually much less trustworthy and much more self-interested than others.

It is only their outstanding abilities in manipulating others that give Machiavellians the reputation of being an intelligent group of people. In reality, there is no verifiable correlation between machs and IQ scores, but the stereotype of the intelligent Machiavellian shifting his or her way through vast webs of action and coming out with everything in mind persists, nevertheless. Emotional intelligence is, however, not a strong point of most Machiavellians. Higher levels of machs are typically correlated with lower EQ scores. Both emotional recognition and emotional empathy are negatively correlated with Machiavellianism. This trait has also never been shown to be correlated to a more advanced theory of mind. This suggests that Machiavellians are not necessarily better able to understand what others are thinking in social situations, so any abilities in manipulation they might possess are not related to their theory of mind.

Chapter3: Case Studies

It may come as a surprise the different ways that dark psychology appears in real life. There are obvious cases of rampant brutality and the will to overpower others. Then there are the more subtle forms that it can present itself. Anyone and everyone are capable of using dark psychology. All it takes is one bad day, or a string of bad days to change someone. Certain "bad apples" are rotten from the start, and can't do anything to change the fact. Not that these individuals are even willing to admit there is something wrong with them. Or that they may even want to change in the first place. Finally, dark psychology applies to those sad cases where people with mental illness could not get the help that they needed and succumbed to the influence of the dark triad. There is no known cure for psychopathy, but several "treatment" options have emerged in clinical psychology. Personality disorders, in general, have targeted by CBT techniques to some success. Changing the behavior patterns and self-image of a psychopath on a fundamental level is difficult for many reasons. For one, within the dark triad, there is the perfect recipe for disaster consisting of self-importance, narcissism and an inflated ego. In other words, the psychopath doesn't want to be cured, unless if by submitting to the treatment they get something out of it, like avoiding jail time or having a reduced sentence.

Dark psychology is responsible for fringe behavior and is often lumped with criminality. Breaking the law, causing bodily or mental harm to others or to self, always finds its way back to dark psychology. Whether it is the desire to hurt someone, use someone for personal gain, revenge or for some other reason. Mental illness seems to be the exception here but may still result in dark psychological tendencies. Suicide, for example, is thought to be caused by depression and doesn't directly relate to dark psychology.

Case: *Murder of Kayla Rolland*

Dark Psychology Involvement: Patterns of child neglect, possibly resulting in psychopathic tendencies

The story of Kayla Roland is a sad one. Up until the Sandy Hook shooting, she was considered the youngest school shooting victim. She was only six and a first grader going to school near Flint, Michigan. One of her classmates, Dederick Owens, was a problem child early on. He reportedly bullied her on previous occasions and was cruel to other students. His many behavioral problems were noted by the school staff, but little was done to correct them. With his father in jail and his mother being a drug addict, he'd had a tough life. Owens brought a small handgun to school one day and shot and killed Kayla Roland in front of the rest of the class.

At the time, Owens was under the custody of his uncle, who ran a drug operation out of his home. Owens was exposed at a very young age to adult violence, drug use, and firearms, which no doubt contributed to his behavior. Normally, young children are excused from having psychopathic diagnoses because of their age (and supposed innocence). But Owens showed the classic signs of psychopathy. He routinely followed Kayla around and wanted to be her friend. In one instance, he attempted to kiss her but was rejected. Just moments before shooting her, Owens told her, "I don't like you" and pulled the trigger.

Here the dark triad is apparent in the Machiavellianism behind the shooting. Owens seemed to be dealing with jealously or some other emotion towards Kayla, which resulted in him acquiring a firearm behind everyone's knowledge and shooting her like it was nothing. Coupled with frequent fights with other students and violent behavior, Owns had all the making of a psychopath. Unfortunately, it was the rotten situation in which he grew up that probably fueled his actions. Guns were easily accessible in the house (he found the handgun under some blankets). And the adults around him normalized violent and anti-social behavior, to the point where murdering a classmate didn't seem so bad.

Case: *Jonestown Massacre*

Dark Psychology Involvement: Cult following, brainwash, deceit, covert manipulation

The Jonestown cult was started by Jim Jones, a charismatic man who opened up to his followers as a guru. They called themselves the Peoples Temple and started a new age religious movement. Jones attracted many people, from all walks of life and religious backgrounds. Paramount to his mission was racial equality, social justice and utopianism. Many found in the Peoples Temple what they could not find in other religious followings. The Temple allowed just about anyone to join as long as they believed in Jone's teachings.

Unfortunately, Jones was a con man from the start. He would schedule fundraising and recruiting events by visiting major cities all across the US with a core group of followers. They would all take Greyhound buses to their destination and invite locals to join them for service. During the service members of the Peoples Temple stood in with the local audience, often outnumbering them by a large amount. Then Jones would perform "cures" on stage, calling up selected followers to act the part of somebody being miraculously cured of their afflictions.

Followers were subjected to all sorts of sexual abuse and psychological brainwashing by their leader. Jones didn't allow members to have sex with another partner inside the church unless they were married, and he frequently had sexual relations with whoever he wished. Many of his followers came from broken homes or were children of abuse. He stood out as a father figure, and it was common that a follower called him "Father."

Jonestown was built by followers hands. They were overworked in the sweaty jungles of Guyana, meanwhile given little to eat and slept odd hours. Jones cut off all informational sources, making him the one stop for news about the world. He convinced his followers of terrible things happening in America and of the possibility of a race war. He also made them believe that their commune would be targeted next. Jones organized a little loyalty test, where he had followers drink from a vat of "poison" that really was just a flavored drink. He told them that the armed forces had landed, and were going to kill them anyways. So they drank. Jones then informed them that it had all been a test, and his followers received praise.

Growing ever more delusional, Jones set up the same trick again, only this time lacing the drink with cyanide poison. Many followers believed it was a test again, but Jones talked about a "revolutionary suicide" on the loudspeakers. Others resisted and had the poison administered by force by Jone's armed personnel. Of those who willingly took the drink, had the poison injected, or thought that it was a test, some 900 died including 300 children.

Case: *Islamic Radicalization*

Dark Psychology Involvement: Brainwash, deceit, covert manipulation

Islamic terrorists are increasingly being radicalized by local terrorist cells abroad. Many of the terrorist attacks in recent years where perpetrated by young men who had an implanted ideology. This can either happen in their home country before leaving or in the host country by local groups. Radicalization works best with younger individuals, usually migrants or refugees who are at odds with the major population. They feel alienated and are either unwilling to assimilate to the new culture or find it incredibly hard to do so.

They then get singled out by religious leaders or terrorist cells who want to recruit them. The usual tools of dark psychological attacks commence. First, the individual is alienated or isolated in the style of the Jonestown victims and fed lies about the people they are ordered to attack. They are told that what they are doing is good and that they will be rewarded for it. Or that by becoming a martyr, they are fighting for the greater good.

Radicalization can happen to just about anyone, given the right toolset and or circumstances. When dark psychology isn't enough, brute force can help turn the tides. That is what happened in 2014 when 148 Kurdish boys and teens were kidnapped by ISIL in Syria. Historical, Kurds and Sunni ISIL fighters do not like each other. Kurdish forces have constant clashes with the terrorist group. But through a blend of propaganda, torture and violence, the Kurdish boys came to accept the teachings of ISIL as true. They believed that their mission was the righteous one, despite being against their own ethnic group.

Case: *Kidnapping and Abuse of Colleen Stan*

Dark Psychology Involvement: abuse, covert manipulation, deceit, kidnap

Colleen was only 20 when she tried hitching a ride from her home in Eugene, Oregon to a friend's house who lived in northern California. A man named Cameron Hooker picked her up. At first appearances, Hooker seemed like a decent person. He was riding with his wife and infant baby in the front. But after they stopped at a gas station, Hooker veered off the highway and put a knife to Stan's throat.

What ensued was a horrific period of seven years where Colleen was subjected to sex slavery and false imprisonment in a coffin-like box. It was reported that she was only allowed a few hours outside of the box daily, was maltreated and used to do Hooker's bidding.

During this time Colleen was also being brainwashed by Hooker, who broke her down emotionally and referred to her only as "K." Hooker was to be addressed as "master" at all times. Colleen was told a fantastic story about an underground organization that would kill her family if she ever tried to escape or resist. And even when Colleen could have escaped or run to the authorities in that seven-year period, she refused to do so. On one occasion, even being allowed to visit her family, Colleen presented Hooker as her boyfriend and said nothing more about it.

There is reason to believe that Hooker was also using dark psychological attacks against his wife, Janice. Janice allowed the abuse to go on because in a way, it absolved her from her previous position as Hooker's sex slave. It is perhaps the main reason why Janice allowed the relationship with the kidnapped girl to go on.

Dark Psychology Spectrum

Common to all these examples is a combination of dark psychology and violence. In the real world, these are extreme and isolated instances of people using dark psychology against others. One is less likely to encounter such extremes in their daily life, but they do outline the underline power, and what may ultimately result from when using dark psychology. Minor interference with dark psychology like trying to get someone fired in the workplace will rarely balloon to criminal offenses.

There is a spectrum between the purely mental and purely violent means to manipulate someone. Kidnapping and then using brainwashing to control the victim lean towards the violent side. This book does not cover the physical side of dark psychology, nor does it touch on instances of physical torture. These are tried and tested methods for breaking someone psychologically but only using physical force. They are routinely used by armed forces against enemies.

Psychopaths may tend towards the violent side if they believe it will get them what they want. Others who dabble with dark psychology, whether intentionally or not, are iffy about crossing the physical violence boundary. And for a good reason, too. Violence is readily accepted as a criminal offense in varying degrees. It also brings up obvious ethical considerations. Such considerations are easier to excuse or ignore if the manipulation is purely non-physical. Though even the ethics of any dark psychological attack are noteworthy, it is up to the attacker whether they think using them is justified.

In the end, it will be up to the court system to decide if such things are ethical. Some techniques on the dark psychology spectrum like blackmail are punishable by law. Most of the time, somebody using dark psychology for bad will be charged under a different, more pressing charge like fraud, extortion, or workplace harassment. In general, any given dark psychology attack is not in and of itself considered a crime.

Key Points

- People who show characteristics that belong to the dark triad are more likely to use dark psychology to manipulate others
- Using dark psychology does not automatically make someone a psychopath or put them under a dark triad classification
- The same underlying techniques that make dark psychology possible can also be used for good
- Dark psychology does not necessarily constitute a crime but may implicate other criminal behavior
- Case studies into who uses dark psychology and why tend to be extreme or sensational in nature. They are what you typically hear on the news. What is more threatening is the type of manipulation you don't hear about.

Things that happen daily in relationships, companies, and out on the streets.

Action Items

1. At some point in your life, you will have to interact with a psychopath. Making up 1% of the population, this much is inevitable. If you live in a city of at least one million, that means there are around 100,000 of these individuals walking around. Some may have a narcissist in their daily lives or somebody who is always scheming. Examine your close and distant relationships for any signs of the dark triad. Is there somebody who is egotistical, overly cruel, or remorseless? If so, do you believe you are currently or have ever been under a dark psychological attack by them?

2. Documentaries, interviews, and news reports are a treasure trove of dark psychology

evidence. Many victims talk about how their captors took away their sense of identity little by little and then started to manipulate them. There is much to learn from these lucky survivors who made it out alive. Pick any of the case studies above or find your own, and watch a few of the first-hand material found online. Who were the people who fell to cults, and why did they do it? How did the scenario affect their lives going forward?

Chapter4: Manipulation

Dark Psychology is all about manipulation. That's its essence. Every Dark Personality, every Dark Trait, almost every Dark Tactic has at its root manipulation.

Manipulation is all around us—through advertising, marketing, from our parents, our supervisors, our lovers, the layout of our local mall. It so completely is a part of our lives we hardly notice it. So when a Psychopath, a Machiavellian approaches us with a request, an ask, a piece of information, no wonder we're not always aware that they're after something. Us, most likely. Or something we have—money, power, our bodies. And we all do it, sometimes it's just a white lie, sometimes flattery, sometimes complete subterfuge. For those of the Dark Triad, however, manipulation is a way of life. They are, to be ungentle about it, predators. And we are their prey.

But let's also be clear about the difference between manipulation and influence. (Influence, it could be argued—that's really what's all around us, via ads and the internet and from our friends and teachers. And subliminal influencing, via subliminal messages, those are definitely covert and underhanded, but used less by individual Dark Personalities and more by governments, advertising, TV, music, and movies—as popularized and demonized in Vance Packard's 1957 classic expose, The Hidden Persuaders, in which Packard claimed that those playing the advertising role used Americans' unconscious needs so that they would buy items they did not desire or even need. Manipulative, for sure. Pathological, no.)

So. The Difference between manipulation and influence. Manipulation often causes confusion, anxiety, depression, and powerlessness. It's unpleasant, it's demeaning. Manipulative relationships are destructive. Manipulators do not care what happens to their targets. Manipulators only want what they want—and the consequences are damned.

People who seek to influence others, they have a positive intent. Their self-esteem does not depend on the actions of the person they are seeking to influence. Influence also involves open and direct communication. The influencer behaves with clarity and transparency and a clear goal, which is usually to the benefit of both parties, if not entirely for the benefit of the person being influenced. And the person being influenced is not just allowed to think for themselves, they're often encouraged to think for themselves and to make their own decisions.

Manipulators lie. They manipulate covertly, indirectly, underhandedly. They feel justified, entitled, rightful to treat others however they choose. Manipulators also see the world in zero-sum terms. Play or get played. Eat or be eaten. The world to them is black and white. For them, a relationship is a power struggle, a connection but one on unequal terms. Terms in their favor, terms they control. Ultimately, they do not trust others—because they know that they themselves are not trustworthy.

Before I begin my attack, I must first become acquainted with her and her whole mental state.

Søren Kierkegaard, The Seducer's Diary

What sort of targets, then, do Manipulators prey on? Do they have a particular type? They do: someone with issues. Unresolved issues. Issues Manipulators can sniff out, then exploit. People struggling with low self-esteem, a good number are naïve, very easy to please, too eager to please, unassertive, lacking in confidence—these are the most vulnerable. People with certain weaknesses like the ones below. If any of these strike a chord, if you have any of these tendencies, any of these behaviors, work on them. Don't try to hide them or hope a Manipulator won't detect them. Work on them. They are:

An unhealthy need to please: The target, fearful of rejection, disapproval, abandonment—of introducing the slightest dose of reality into the relationship—keeps everything as pleasant as possible.

Sometimes the urge of feeling the need to earn that very approval and acceptance from other people: Sometimes corresponds to a lack of confidence in one's own judgments—especially of others. Especially when it comes to Manipulators—who put on a very convincing front but to a target, often just feel off. But without a solid sense of self, the target yields to others. This need for approval can then cloud one's trust in oneself, in one's visceral reaction to a Manipulator.

Cannot say No!: Or just No, thank you. A lack of assertiveness, especially, again, when it comes to one's feelings or one's own needs or wants.

Soft personal boundaries: A murky sense of who you are. Your identity rests too much in others and you tend to merge or lose yourself in another person's boundaries. A person just one step up from soft, who has spongy boundaries is, according to Old Dominion professor by the name Nina Brown, known as an author of Coping With Infuriating, Critical People—Call them Destructive Narcissistic Pattern, Mean, someone with soft and rigid boundaries. People with soft boundaries are not sure of who to open up to and who to keep out.

Low self-reliance: You tend to cling to others and rely on them and can even see them as superior or more powerful. You're emotionally dependent, submissive.

Fear of negative emotions: You cannot express anger, frustration, or disapproval. What Harriet B. Braiker, author of The Disease To Please, calls "emotophobia."

The feeling that an individual doesn't feel in control and that more so everything is someone else's fault: If the situation of being in the drivers seat is the degree to which an individual will believe they have the power of the resulting outcome of events in the pattern of their lives, people with an external locus of control blame (or thank) outside factors for what happens in their lives.

And two others: the overly conscientious—targets who are ever willing to provide the Manipulator the satisfaction of the benefit of the doubt—more so the over-intellectualizer—the target who is intent on figuring out why it is the Manipulator continues to do the things they do, all the while staying with the Manipulator rather than leaving.

Whether or not you are on this list, being manipulated is not your fault. Manipulators know what they're doing. They are in control. The manipulated, though, until they see it, they have little idea what's going on. Even so, it is still up to the target of the Manipulator to put up boundaries. That is not victim blaming, it's just how it is. The Manipulator will not stop until their target puts a stop to their behavior. Otherwise, there's no incentive. Things are working out great for them; they're getting exactly what they want. Why stop? The solution: Stop rewarding their tactics. Manipulation exists because it works.

The techniques of manipulation are many—and seemingly endless. Here are some—some of the ones used most often by Dark Personality types.

Love Bombing (aka Love Flooding): Unlike the display of a healthy romantic level of interest, Love Bombing happens too fast and comes on way too strong. The Manipulator immediately want to spend every moment with you; they're madly in love with you right there at the bar, in the middle of happy hour.

According to Michael Pace, author of Dark Psychology, Mind Games, And Other Tricks Of The Trade including Brainwashing, Love bombing has almost nothing to do with love. It's all a ruse—the early stage of the Manipulator readying his victim.

Positive Reinforcement: After the Love Bombing comes positive reinforcement, which comes in many forms, from outright praise and superficial charm straight to superficial sympathy as they say (crocodile tears) and exceedingly apologizing. As Dark Psychology author Michael Pace explains it, this comes soon after the Love Bombing. Only it's hardly at all positive. Instead, the Manipulator has stopped Love Bombing altogether and replaced it with . . . crickets. For instance, the target must wear a certain dress the Manipulator gave them before the Manipulator will give them a kiss. The target has no idea that the kiss comes not from the

Manipulator's desire for her, it's because he coerced her into doing what he wanted.

Negative Reinforcement: Even though that behavior is not deliberate, the Manipulator uses negative reinforcement to get you, the target, to adopt to his wishes, his demands—no matter how unreasonable.

Love Denial/Love Withdrawal: First he Giveth, then he Taketh away. After all that love, the Manipulator lets the target know just who's boss by withdrawing all that love and attention and affection. If the Manipulator doesn't out-and-out leave, their love its quality, its frequency, its expression morphs into something altogether . . . different. As if you have less value than the day before they professed their undying love for you.

Diversion: The Manipulator won't give you a clear and straight answer, even to questions that need a No or Yes answer, and instead often drives the conversation to some another topic.

Evasion: Just like Diversion but now the Manipulator gives unclear, rambling, and irrelevant responses—weasel words—words or even statements that are seemingly intentional when it comes to misleading or ambiguous. Shaming is and can be subtle to a disappointed look, a tone of voice, a mean glance—and mostly they are hugely effective at bringing that very sense or thought of inadequacy in the given target.

Vilifying the Victim: This is mostly used by the Manipulator as another way of getting over their guilt over some wrongdoing they've committed, this is when and how the Manipulator depicts someone else in the worst possible light in order to justify their own behaviors. It's a rather ingenious way of creating confusion about who the real target is. They falsely blame others to shirk free of any responsibility or accountability for their actions. I slept with your best friend but you pushed me into it. Worse, if the target defends themselves or their position, the Manipulator, in response, falsely accuses the target as being the abuser.

Projecting Blame (Blaming Others): Manipulators are so effective because unless they work in such subtle, hard-to-detect, nearly impossible to explain ways. Projecting blame, where the Manipulator scapegoats the target, is particularly insidious. A combination of misdirection and blame-shifting, the Manipulator casts their flaws and feelings onto the target: "I was late for an important meeting because you said I had to pick up the kids." Projecting blame is repeatedly a way of psychological plus emotional manipulations. Manipulators often do lie about lying, to continuously manipulate and re-manipulate the original, the less believable kind of a story into a realistically "more acceptable" that the target will definitely believe to be the truth. Another tactic is visualizing lies to being the truth. Manipulators often love to point accusing figures falsely to accuse theire target as if they deserve to be treated in that manner. Manipulators will often point solidly and claim that their target is crazy or even abusive, (See Feigning, below.)

Moving the Goalposts: You might think you know where you stand with a Manipulator, but if they are constantly moving the goalposts in order to confuse you, then it's likely you're dealing with a predator. The ground is always shifting. One day the Manipulator tells you to leave the lights on, the next day he berates you for not having turned the lights off.

Gaslighting: A nefarious tactic, akin to brainwashing. The Manipulator makes the target to believe and to doubt themself, and eventually lose her very own thought and sense of perception, talk of self-worth and most of all identity. The Manipulator: C'mon. I never told you that. Or: You're being paranoid. Or: Why are you making such a big deal out of this?

Feigning Innocence/Ignorance: The Manipulator, playing the innocence card, draws an illustration to suggest that every harm done was not intentional or in other words what they are accused of never happened. The target feels like a false accuser, a perpetrator, and often questions their judgment and their sanity.

Feigning Confusion: Manipulator pretend to be dumb, making it look as if they do not have an idea of what the target is actually talking about or even pretend they are confused and not focused about an important issue being brought to their knowledge. You even find the Manipulator having to intentionally confuse the target to purposely make the target doubt their own sense of the accuracy of their perception, mostly to point out the key elements the Manipulator indeed intentionally included just there is a reason to doubt.

Brandishing Anger: Manipulator brings anger to play, the intensity of emotional, and aggressiveness to shock and make the target panic resulting into submission. In this case you find that the Manipulator is actually not angry, this is just a false act. The aggressiveness "anger" is mostly and highly effective as a way in which the Manipulator uses to avoid telling what is actually the truth at those inconvenient moments and/or circumstances; the target—scared, uncertain if the anger is genuine or not—becomes more focused on the anger instead of either the original topic or the tactics of manipulation.

Bandwagon Effect: The Manipulator uses their bag of tricks by pretending to comfort the target to actually submit by making it seem like they are claiming whether it's true or false that other people are doing it, so you can too. It mostly surfaces in situations where the Manipulator does always try to influence their target into trying different things like for example sexual acts or drugs.

In the case of such scenarios or behaviors hits a nerve, there's manipulation going on. And the only real way to stop the manipulation from continuing is to stop falling into the manipulation. Don't fool yourself into thinking that if the Manipulator knew better they would treat you better. The more victimized you feel, the less you will feel able to powerful over yourself or your life. As you become more diminished, you to change the manipulator, focus on changing you and your behavior.

Chapter 5: NLP (Neuro-Linguistic Programming)

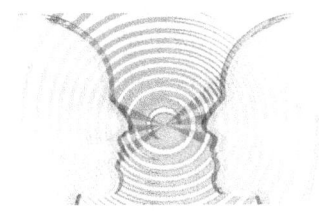

What is hypnosis?

This is just the way that people may use hypnosis to influence people around them without their knowledge. This can be thought of as 'covert hypnosis'. It may not always be as hard to detect and malevolent as most people might think. However, its power and widespread influence should never be underestimated.

This involves avoiding the critical thinking portions of the brain and embedding ideas in the deeper parts of the mind that we don't consciously control. While most people will innocently use a lot of these techniques without realizing it, there are those who know exactly what they are doing and intentionally using them on unsuspecting people.

Who is most likely to use it on you?

We come across covert hypnosis all the time without realizing it. While it can't be used to brainwash and mind-control people the way you see on stage or in the movies, it's still a powerful tool for gaining the compliance of people around you.

One will come across it most often in everyday life when advertisers want to get you to buy something. They want your money, not your consent. To this end, they research ways to get you to comply and give them your money without asking questions.

Other people in power who want unquestioned followers will use these techniques as well, like televangelists and politicians.

Tactics

Dominate the subject's attention

The reason you are most likely to see hypnotism used on you while you watch television or surf the web is because that is when you are fully engrossed in what you are doing and are in an attentive state of mind that leaves you highly suggestible.

When someone has your full attention to the point where time seems to fly and everything else seems to matter a bit less is when they have the most power over you. This is when you're more likely to register the things they say on a deeper level than you usually do, to the point of not thinking critically about what they were saying.

Think of the last time you were enjoying a book or conversation to the point where time flew by you. How much time do you think you spent engaging your critical mind to question what was going on and fact check?

Engage imagination

Taking someone on an imaginative journey to some special place in their minds where they are more likely to feel safe is where they are more likely to be open to influence and suggestion. You'll often find hypnotherapists and other types of hypnotists using a method that applies to this principle.

This is because the imagination is a powerful tool. If you can get someone to picture themselves doing something and not regretting it for any reason, then you open them up to a new world where a new option is open to them. As long as the target feels safe and in control then they won't even realize their imagination is being used against them.

Soft commands

This is a great way to bypass the critical part of the brain that registers things like right and wrong. This is more likely to work because trying to give a hard command like, "you will lose weight" is less likely to activate any resistance from the critical part of the brain. You will have better chances with a soft command like, "how jealous will your ex be once you've lost weight?"

The brain often doesn't even register this as a command and will focus on the part it finds the most appealing. Just listen to commands that require you to do something without actually asking your consent about whether you want to do said something. This makes you think the idea was all yours when it was actually placed there by someone else.

Linking presupposition

This one is a bit trickier to pull off than one would expect as it requires more finesse than most people are willing to practice to muster. It involves a lot of different elements and can have a lot of moving parts, but can be useful to learn to spot or even use.

Linking presupposition involves asking someone to do something that seems to line up with what they were going to do anyway. Think of someone suggesting you add some special package on a car you're buying even though you may not need it. Sounds familiar right? That's because it is.

When done right, it can make people take on more than they had initially intended. One simply needs to get someone to imagine that taking that small extra step won't do any harm when they were already headed in that direction anyway.

Reality stacking

You will often find politicians and seducers doing this. It involves getting people emotional about things they agree with and then slotting their own agendas in there as if it was a natural extension of the discussion that was missing until just then.

Once you have someone feeling relaxed in the thought that they understand where you're coming from and then aligning yourself with the ideas they carried all along then they will be more likely to see you or your suggestion linking to their ideas as plausible and maybe even natural. You will often hear advertisers doing something similar, especially when advertising for a pharmaceutical company.

The realities don't actually have to have that strong a link to begin with. Just get people saying 'yes' enough times and they will want to keep saying it because it continues a trend.

Trends are easier to follow than they are to break, so they'll likely just keep going with it.

Strongly descriptive language

This isn't inherently bad. It's often used by a lot of people when they are trying to tell a really good story. However, there are those who know that the minds love of descriptive knowledge is the quickest path past their logical brain and right to their emotional brain.

It is common for parents to use this language to explain tricky concepts to children since it is easier to understand. On the other hand, it can also be used by manipulators (like lawyers and dark seducers) to get people to believe them without asking too many questions.

Answering a question or telling a story with as much descriptive language as possible will make someone think that they are being told the truth and want to follow the emotional content of the story more than the intellectual content. This is the power of painting word pictures in people's' minds.

Hidden suggestion

The tactic of hiding a suggestion relies on subtle plays on words that might register as a slip of the tongue or the target simply mishearing what was being said. This is more of a one-on-one trick than anything else and requires you to pay attention in case it isn't as innocent as one may think.

The hidden suggestion involves sliding a suggestion in the place of something that sounds very similar. Almost mumbling words like 'die' in the place of words like 'dine' will slowly ingrain the idea of death in someone's mind. It doesn't have to be the said every time, but enough times that it starts to settle in the victim's mind.

Catching someone doing this will not always be easy as they can turn the tables on you and say that they aren't saying it and you must actually have it on your mind if you keep hearing it.

Tone/language mimicry

A dark hypnotist can, in a one-on-one setting, listen out for some of the words a target uses the most when they are feeling a certain way. They can then use them against them when they are trying to invoke certain emotions to lower their opponent's guard and make them more compliant.

This can also be done with vocal tone. If someone memorizes how your voice changes when you say certain things then they can mimic that tone of voice to make people gradually open up to wanting to listen to them when they say particular things in that specific tone.

The ideas said in those moments will feel more like they come from the mind of the target more than they do from the mouth of the manipulator.

Environmental stimulus

A manipulator can open a target to being more agreeable by making it a point to associate certain places with certain emotions. For example, they can give you a small gift every time you pass a certain place until your mind comes to expect it. Once your mind has linked that place with receiving a gift then you are more likely to take on a receptive attitude when you are near that place.

It can also be used to put things in a certain environment that trigger unpleasant emotions. They may put certain things, like images of snakes, in the background of places they want you to feel fear in. Once they have the feelings triggered, they can use the emotional state they induced to slowly change your perception of certain things.

Engage all the senses

Hypnosis works well when it engages as many senses as possible. Once the mind is too busy being engaged on multiple levels, then it starts to lose the ability to focus on detecting threats. Your full attention needs to be where the hypnotist needs it to be.

So when they use words to engage your senses, then your mind becomes too preoccupied to think too hard on things like right and wrong. The heightened state of awareness pointed in another direction makes it easier to subtly plant ideas into the mind of an unsuspecting target.

It relies on the same fundamental principles that are used in magic tricks, pick-pocketing and even martial arts. It's the old story of the magic trick not being where you're looking.

NLP

NLP, which is short for Neuro-Linguistic Programming, is a practice that studies how people map out the world around them in their minds. It also studies how to read these maps people make in their minds and remap them where and when it is necessary. The people who put these kinds of ideas and techniques together were Richard Bandler and John Grinder back in 1975.

While it may use a lot of techniques found in hypnosis, it is important to note that NLP is not hypnosis. It merely draws on the scientific elements of hypnosis, along with many other practices, in an attempt to create a structured way to gain power over 'the voices on their heads' and change their lives.

NLP is widely used by many professionals in high-pressure jobs as well as life coaches in order to get the best out of one's mind in the least harmful ways possible. Many successful people who have used (or still use) NLP will attest to the power of reprogramming one's thoughts and using the mind as a tool to better oneself. However, NLP can also have a very dark side.

Because of the power of self-awareness can create in one's own mind to control themselves, it can also give dark personalities the power to control others. This becomes possible when you realize that the tactics used in NLP can covertly be used on other people once a person becomes adept enough at using them.

State Calibration

State calibration is when one pays very close attention to the person, or people, they are interacting with. They look for the smallest changes in body language. Being well versed in how to read moods and emotions through facial expressions and body language, a person will use this information to change their own state in a way that keeps the other person under their influence.

This touches on the subject of mirroring and works best while still building rapport and deepening the bond one has with a target. Having enough understanding of how thoughts and feelings affect body language can help a neuro-linguistic programmer who knows what they are doing to keep matching or complimenting a person's moods with their own.

Using state calibration well can be a powerful way to build a deep bond with someone and get them in a more trusting mood. Since most people only partially give their attention to people, a target may register this deep reading as the persuader being interested in them to the point of giving them their full attention.

People are more likely to like people they are convinced likes them.

On top of building rapport, knowing how to analyze like this may help better detect how someone feels about you, someone else or even themselves. It can also help tell if someone is being deceitful as the moods of most people will change very slightly when they lie.

Anchoring

This is a technique that draws directly from hypnosis. It involves linking a certain emotion to a specific gesture, pose, motion, object, etc. It can be used on oneself or their opponent. It does not have to be negative, but one will see how it can take on darker tones when used by the wrong person.

Anchoring oneself usually begins by getting into a hypnotic trance (it can be done alone or with the help of a skilled practitioner). Once they are here, the hypnotist will ask them to recall a memory that induced a certain emotional state. Once they are in that state they will try to amplify that emotional state by getting them to recall as many sensory memories as they can. This is when they will help them to tie those feelings to a movement or gesture, etc. That chosen pose or gesture will be their anchor. Once this is complete, a person will be able to feel those emotions again by using that anchor when they need to.

If this calls back memories of Pavlov's experiment with conditioning dogs to certain stimuli, then you will be recalling right. This technique draws directly from the findings in that study, which becomes the reason it can be so dark. In the wrong hands, it can be used to train someone to change their feelings towards certain behaviors and adopt different ones.

Frame Control

This can be a simple to use tool that can be powerful during debates and negotiations. While it may have been touched on in earlier chapters, this will now be when the reader will come to a better understanding of how it works.

Controlling the frame is basically presenting an idea in a certain way. Controlling the frame in a conversation or thought pattern is referred to as reframing. An example of how this works is if someone gives you two choices. They are presenting the frame (the operative ideas) of the conversation. Since they presented it, they control it.

How would one then gain control of the frame? By reframing it. This can take the form of introducing a third option into the conversation (if we to stick to the previous example) that the other person will now have to consider. So the person who presents the frame controls it, but the other one can regain it by reframing it.

Dissociation

This is a visualization technique that can help someone overcome negative emotions during stressful situations. Psychopaths are often successful liars because they naturally disassociate their emotions from their actions, so they can be completely calm while lying, even when they know they've been caught.

Dissociation, for people who aren't that high in dark personality traits, will have to be done consciously as our brain's chemistry might often work against us when we most need it to be calm. A good example of how to practice this is to picture yourself outside of your body when facing a stressful situation. Observe the object of your stress and try switch your roles. Imagine what may be going through the mind of the person you want to seduce, or the boss you're trying to get to like you.

If one wanted to take dissociation a step further, they could turn around and observe themselves. Picture seeing oneself from outside the body and then act as if the body is acting completely separate from the mind and emotions. One can even go as far as to pretend they can control their body remotely while being outside it.

Mapping across

Mapping across is a tactic that falls somewhere between hypnosis and meditation. It can be done to one oneself or another person.

This technique involves using future visualization to make someone more likely to take certain action in the future under certain circumstances. It involves registering one's emotions about a certain event that will happen in the future and how they will want to react to it. After this, one can then consider how they feel about it deep down at that current point. The last step is to steadily replace the current feelings with the feelings one will want to feel in the possible world of that future even.

So if someone is afraid of something they have to do in the future, they can focus more on how they will feel once that event has taken place and passed. If they keep their focus on the feelings that will come after the event has passed, then their minds will learn to register those feelings rather than the negative ones they may currently feel towards it. By the time the event comes to pass, they will have been programmed (by themselves or others) to feel a certain way about the event which will increase the chances that they will do even better since they won't be going in with negative emotions.

Eliminating bad thoughts

Many people are usually held back from what they want because of negative thoughts that are the result of something that took place sometime in their past and has embedded itself into their subconscious minds.

There are three simple steps one can learn to use to prevent themselves from being overtaken by negative thoughts and act as they want rather than acting as their past dictates they act. The three techniques a person can use to do away with negative thoughts are:

Make bad thoughts intentional

While the natural intuition is to avoid thinking bad thoughts altogether, this may play against someone who is prone to neuroticism and other such negative thoughts.

By actively seeking out the bad thoughts and the memories that may automatically play out in one's head, you train your brain to recognize that you are actually the one who is in control of these thoughts. Over time, you will become desensitized to these negative thoughts. And the feelings attached to them.

Remember thought nature

When you catch yourself distracted by bad thoughts, it may be helpful to pause and observe the thought and its effects on you. When you've identified whether it helps or not, you can tell yourself 'it's just a thought' and dismiss it. Switch your mind to a more helpful or positive thought.

When you keep doing this, you realize that your mind is just a tool that you use and control, not the other way around.

Wash them out : Another method to help rid oneself of negative thoughts is to try to wash them out as they occur. Simply identify a negative thought you want to be free of. Make it as vivid and clear as you possibly can. Once you have, allow the colors to go a dull white and the volume to steadily fade.

Do this with the same thought over and over and you will find that it will become harder and harder to recall it at all.

Chapter6: How to defend from people with the dark side of personality: narcissism, sadism, etc...

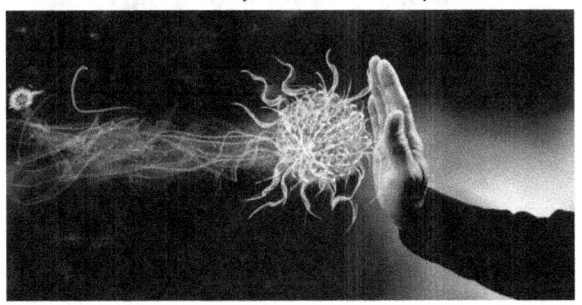

Narcissism

At its most basic, narcissism describes a sense of extreme entitlement, lack of empathy, and excessive admiration of oneself. The word comes from a Greek myth of Narcissus, where by a young man that was so handsome who apparently fell in love with himself by looking at his own reflection. He was callous and condescending towards those who loved him and drove some to commit suicide to prove their undying admiration of him. There are many signs an individual is narcissistic, and you have most likely met someone who displays this personality trait.

One of the most obvious signs of a narcissist is an excessive preoccupation with how they are perceived by others. They may spend an excessive amount of time grooming themselves and constantly presenting themselves in a light so positive that it treads on dishonest. The narcissist wants to be seen as a fabulous human being, constantly living it up and showing off their success and importance. They may exaggerate their achievements, social climb, or name drop about which important people they rub shoulders with.

In addition, a narcissist is an arrogant person who believes themselves to be more capable, important, and worthy than those around them. They are often exploitative and lacking in empathy, which means that they will use others to get what they want, with no mind that it may be hurtful to the victim. Narcissists are able to do this because they view others as extensions of themselves and are unable to fathom that others have priorities that are dissimilar to their own—no favor is too big to ask for, and the narcissist's self-centeredness makes them believe that they are justified in their actions. The narcissist believes his or her needs are above those of others—why shouldn't others be extra considerate of them.

Think you've seen anger? Just wait until you meet narcissistic rage. As explained in the above chapters Narcissistic anger or rage is the result of a narcissistic injury. A narcissistic injury afflicts a narcissistic person when their grandiose opinion of themselves is challenged or shown to be faulty. For example, a narcissistic injury can come from being rejected by a potential romantic partner or getting turned down from a job. Having this easily triggered response to rejection and disappointment frequently is the result of childhood trauma, such as a neglectful or abusive parent. The child, who senses that their parent does not love them, developed a grandiose persona in order to hide their deep feelings of inadequacy and shame, and to convince themselves that they will be invulnerable to such suffering at the hands of another ever again. Essentially, the narcissist is constantly trying to cover up how insecure they really feel by pretending they are the greatest, most fabulous and accomplished human being of all time.

Once the injury occurs, the narcissist may fly into what is known as the narcissistic rage. They will be unable to regulate their emotions and actions. The actions resulting from narcissistic rage can range anywhere from the silent treatment and temporarily withdrawing from others all the way to physical violence and serious abuse. Narcissistic rage occurs because the narcissistic injury is simply too much to bear. To the narcissist, it calls into question how great they actually and exposes them as imperfect beings.

There are many telltale signs of a narcissist and knowing some of their common behavior can make them easier to spot. For one thing, they will take credit for good things that happen to them, and blame bad outcomes on others, no matter what the reality of the situation is. If they get a bad grade on a project, they will insist that the professor has it out for them or that the grading process was unfair. If they have a good outcome, say someone of their preferred sex being friendly, they may insist this person was flirting with them. The narcissist wants to bend every story to present themselves in the most positive light and will not entertain any possibility that they may be wrong about something.

A narcissistic person is also obsessed with perfection. Not only do they hold themselves to high standards, which they often believe themselves to meet, but they also hold entities external to themselves to such a standard. The narcissist expects the people around them to behave perfectly, for events they attend to be perfect, and their circumstances to be perfect. They will become irate if they feel others have not met their expectations, even if they are unreasonable.

Another sign you may be dealing with a narcissist is that they speak in extremes about those around them. For example, they may profess how "special" you are and how much they love you one day, but as soon as you irritate them, they will disparage, insult, or neglect you. Despite a close relationship, a narcissist will always seem fairly uninterested in you as a person. You may tell them you had a bad day, or an interesting story about your day, and they will respond by talking about themselves. We have all had conversations like this—it's almost jarring. There you are, drinking coffee with a friend and believing both yours and your friend's needs hold equal weight in the conversation, when they suggest otherwise by talking about themselves nonstop. They will ask you a few questions about yourself and if they do, they seem to lose interest once you being to reply. In short, what's the biggest sign someone is a narcissist? A narcissist will make you wonder if their life motto is "It's all about me!"

Machiavellianism

Before we get into Machiavellianism, let us understand the word's namesake, Niccolò Machiavelli. Nicolò Machiavelli was an Italian statesman during the Italian renaissance during the fifteenth and sixteenth centuries. He was a diplomat, politician, secretary, philosopher, poet, historian, humanist and playwright. He is known today for his book, "Il Principe," or "The Prince." The book is a deep analysis of maintenance and possession of political power, written so Machiavelli could return to Italian politics from exile and hopefully be appointed a political advisory position by the Medici family. The book was so shocking at the time that Machiavelli was labelled and atheist. Machiavelli advocated for ruthless, cunning, and strategic methods of gaining and keeping political power. He is often credited with the saying, "the ends justify the means."

Given this introduction of Machiavelli the man, a deeper discussion of Machiavellianism as a member of the dark triad is appropriate. Machiavellianism includes low empathy, prioritizing power over others, strong ambition, and exploitation of others for personal gain. Machiavellianism is different from psychopathy because of the Machiavellian's emphasis on exploitation for personal gain, whereas a psychopath's very nature is insensitivity and callousness no matter what.

The Machiavellian believes human nature is inherently evil, and that deception is a justifiable way to attain goals and success. They generally undervalue human connection and overvalue wealth and power. The believe depending on others and cultivating meaningful emotional relationships is a worthless endeavor. When they manipulate or exploit others, they believe they have acted with reason and can justify their actions. They will do something terrible to complete a goal and when confronted, they will say, "Hey, I got the job done, right? It all worked out."

So, how do you know you're dealing with a Machiavellian? The Machiavellian is notoriously low on empathy; human connection always comes second to achievement and personal gain. To the Machiavellian, people are often conduits to other things—money, power, sex, or whatever else may seem worthwhile to achieve. Machiavellians are known to lie and exploit when necessary in order to get what they want.

Another common quality of Machiavellians is their penchant for strategy and calculation. A Machiavellian is good at sizing up others. They can read the room so to speak, and are perceptive of others' thoughts, feeling and weaknesses, despite the low empathy that accompanies Machiavellianism. Due to this calculating nature, these people tend to be patient. They are constantly collecting information and analyzing it to use to their best advantage. They know how to plan and wait for their rewards.

The demeanor of a Machiavellian often falls into one of two camps. They either seem aloof and emotionally distant or charming and friendly. Note that both of these demeanors may be present in the same person; someone may be charming and friendly but reveal so little about themselves that you may become suspicious or realize well into a relationship of any kind with the Machiavellian that you know little about them. This is deliberate, as the Machiavellian generally prefers not to share their true intentions with others.

With respect to their morals, Machiavellians are unlike psychopaths. While the psychopath simply lacks morals, the Machiavellian's are scattered, inconsistent, and ill-defined. The Machiavellian may claim to have certain ethical principles they value highly, but they are certainly willing to ignore them if they can justify doing so. Generally speaking, they have little respect for humanity as a whole. They think it is inherently evil, or at the very least not good, and are usually cynical.

Sadism

It's a bit of a given that most if not all people have sadistic thoughts, or have a little bit of a sadist in them. This does not, obviously, qualify everyone as a sadist, or even a latent sadist (even when given the right opportunity—as proven by psychologist Philip Zimbardo in his 1971 Stanford prison experiment, in which Stanford undergraduates took part as prisoners and guard in a mock prison, and soon proved that people are only too easily persuaded to inflict pain on others, and others are only too eager to submit to such authoritarian cruelty. It has been documented that we humans are naturally driven by instincts towards cruelty and aggression).

Nevertheless, humans aggress. Humans kill their own species—and often without reason or cause, and sometimes solely for pleasure. As far as cruelty goes, as it relates to Sadism, humans also appear to have a fascination with the spectacle of violence, either as participants or viewers. This fascination seems to transcend time and culture. Humans, not all but plenty, derive pleasure out of seeing others hurt. It could be argued that there's a potential Everyday Sadist lurking in all of us, but guilt, conscience, circumstance, context, whatever, keeps it tamped down. Or hidden.

Going by the conjectures, then the character of motivation to inflict struggling may actually be present in all humans, and the only major difference or contrast between the non-sadists and sadists narrows down to the latter group that has found the tactic to conquer their inward cruelty.

As to Everyday Sadist, a sadistic personality can center on many things. The will, as some researchers have said, maligning and humiliating, to practice absolute power with no restricted control or supervision over another, or the ecstasy brought up from other people's suffering. Sadists like to intentionally cause psychological pain, suffering or even sexual, purposely for their own benefits.

The enjoyment of the sadistic act can come via direct participation (core sadism) or not so directly, such as watching others inflict pain and suffering (vicarious sadism). The late American psychologist Theodore Millon proposed four types of sadism: explosive sadism, enforcing sadism, tyrannical sadism and spineless sadism,. The Everyday Sadist might have the traits of one or all four of these types, though each of these subtypes tend to stay within their personality traits. According to Millon's definition, the Spineless Sadist is insecure, cowardly, tend to swagger and brag, and picks out powerless scapegoats as targets. The Tyrannical Sadist loves to menace and brutalize others, hoping for their submission, cuts people down verbally, is accusatory and destructive, and tends to be surly, abusive, and inhumane; in a word: a bully, whether in person or online (internet trolls are largely Tyrannical Sadists). The Enforcing Sadist are usually police officers, bossy supervisors, deans, judges, those who sublimate their hostility into the larger good, and therefore as public servants, profess the right to act harshly; they like to control and punish, and feel it their duty to ferret out rule breakers. The Explosive Sadist has a deep reservoir of bottled-up and often uncontrollable rage, and is prone to unpredictable and violent physical and verbal outbursts, only to later show contrition.

The Everyday Sadist can be any one of these Sadist subtypes. And true Sadists experience a kind of rush, repeatedly, whenever hurting others, and often, they lack the appropriate level of conscience needed to keep their addiction to sadistic pleasure under control.

Below are some of the more common outward traits of the typical Everyday Sadist.

They enjoy seeing people hurt and suffering. This could mean anything—from starting a rumor to publicly shaming someone, all just so they can watch that person squirm, and know that they caused that person their pain.

They enjoy hurting people. They enjoy bringing physical harm and pain to others. For example, this particular Sadist is standing in line at the movies. They don't like that the person behind them is standing too close, so they accidentally stomp on that person's foot.

They get excited by the idea of knowing others are in pain. A fight breaks out on the sidewalk. The Sadist doesn't shy away or call for help. They're right there, glued to the action. The violence, especially the suddenness of it, appeals to them.

They think it is acceptable to cause others' pain. Taking a kind of nihilistic, Hobbesian do or be done to approach to life, Sadists espouse a kind of affectless acceptance of kill or be killed. Hurt others before, or lest, they hurt you. Either way, they're OK with it.

They fantasize about hurting others. Sadists can drift off to thoughts of torture, mayhem, revenge fantasies, cruel sexual fantasies—all with a smile on their face.

They hurt others because they can. Squashing bugs seems OK. But when it's just for pleasure—that's sadistic. Similarly, Sadists think it's OK to bully others, and lately, they think it's especially OK to do it anonymously, online, where there are almost no consequences.

They like being humiliating others in order to keep them in line. If you're engaged in an argument with a Sadist, don't be surprised if they go from their inside voice to their outside voice in seconds—all the better to draw the attention of others and put you into an uncomfortable, embarrassing position.

Their sexual tendencies have an edge to them. If they want you to submit to sexual acts such as bondage, gagging, slapping, hair pulling, choking.

Conclusion

While many will assume they know the dark underbelly of humanity, they do not. They only learn what their own lives have conditioned them to see. They see what their individual histories may dictate they see. They often don't realize that they often see what others want them to see.

We all create an illusion about ourselves, our situations, maybe even our realities. We chose to live in them and portray them as true because it can often make life easier to bear. We do the things we do, not intending on hurting anyone around us. In most cases, you will find that there is usually little to no malice in the words of most people in a civilized society. They go about their business doing the best that they can. Unfortunately, not all of humanity operates like this.

There are people in history, and some living among us today, who seemed have had a natural proclivity for doing what seems unnatural. They operate in ways that seem to baffle the minds of the rest of the population. They can even do things that can turn the stomachs of many decent people.

In order to help dispel some of the mysteries behind the ways of these people, you were shown how they can be a part of our everyday lives as lawyers, leaders, salesmen, public speakers, celebrities, etc. The essence of their very techniques was gutted and presented to you as honestly as possible.

On top of everything you had already learned about dark psychology, you were shown some of the other tactics dark persuaders may use against you in some unexpected settings. This all happened while a clear division between people who use this on purpose and by mistake was maintained as to avoid creating unnecessary suspicion and paranoia, especially in more sensitive readers. The journey would only get darker from there.

While you dove into the personality traits of these kinds of people, you were given a lot of insight into what makes people who can be considered as having 'dark personalities' tick. Hopefully, you have gained valuable knowledge regarding how these people may operate. Perhaps you even learned about the best ways to adopt some of these stratagems for your own benefit. How you use them is completely up to you.

One of the greatest tools in changing your own life for the better is learning to read people. Knowing the way other people communicate is a great way to improve one's own communication skills without saying a word. That is why it was imperative that you learn how you can read others because others are always reading you.

Bibliography/Sources
References

Derry McClean. Filtering on Psychological control and manipulation. Journal of psychology control and social beings.

Ken Wilber. Classification of different ways of coping with psychological manipulation. Forbidden psychology.

Edward Benedict. Techniques in dark psychology influencing humans and mind control.

www.ingramcontent.com/pod-product-compliance
Lightning Source LLC
Chambersburg PA
CBHW071800080526
44589CB00012B/629